CHELSEA
CHELSEA
BANG BANG

OTHER BOOKS STARRING
CHELSEA HANDLER

Lies Chelsea Handler Told Me

CHELSEA CHELSEA BANG BANG

Chelsea Handler

GRAND CENTRAL
PUBLISHING

NEW YORK   BOSTON

Photographs on pages 80, 94, 155, and 238 © Eva Magdelenski.
Photograph on page 151 © Paul Reder.
Photograph on page 227 © Sue Murphy.
All other photographs are courtesy of the author.

Grand Central Publishing
Hachette Book Group
237 Park Avenue
New York, NY 10017

www.HachetteBookGroup.com

Printed in the United States of America

Originally published in hardcover by Grand Central Publishing.

First Trade Edition: September 2011
10 9 8 7 6 5 4 3 2 1

Grand Central Publishing is a division of Hachette Book Group, Inc.
The Grand Central Publishing name and logo is a trademark of Hachette Book Group, Inc.

The publisher is not responsible for websites (or their content) that are not owned by the publisher.

The Library of Congress has cataloged the hardcover edition as follows:

Handler, Chelsea.
    Chelsea Chelsea bang bang / Chelsea Handler.—1st ed.
       p. cm.
    ISBN 978-0-446-55244-8
    1. Women—Humor.   2. American wit and humor.
3. Man-woman relationships—Humor.   I. Title.
    PN6231.W6H27 2010
    814'.6—dc22
                                                    2009044846

ISBN 978-0-446-55243-1 (pbk.)

To my brothers and sisters.
What . . . a bunch of assholes.

CHELSEA
CHELSEA
BANG BANG

Chapter One

The Feeling

I was eight years old and well into the third grade at Riker Hill Elementary School when I fell head over heels in love with myself. What can only be described as the "cornerstone of my youth" came unexpectedly out of left field and washed over me like a Category 5 cyclone. Not enough to drown me completely, but enough for me to lose my footing and knock me on my supple eight-year-old ass.

A friend of mine named Stacy Silverberg invited me to a sleepover party at her house, where she was going to teach everyone how to get "the feeling." I had never heard of the feeling before, but it was definitely something that piqued my interest. Reason led me to assume it had something to do with either a Smurf or a Cabbage Patch Kid, both of varying appeal.

When I got to Stacy's house, her Jamaican housekeeper, Margaret—or, as I liked to call her, M-Dawg—let me in. Stacy's parents were always out on the town, and her house was always spotless, which was a nice respite from the doughnut-stained, dog-hair-covered sofas my parents tried to pass off as sanitary.

When I walked into Stacy's room, there were a total of four girls already there, all facedown on their sleeping bags with their clothes on, violently rubbing their vaginas. I was appalled that no one had the good manners to manage a hello and equally taken aback by the pure ecstasy on all their faces.

I had never planted my face so fast into a carpet in my life. This was what my brother Greg referred to as a "double *jackpot.*"

"Over my jeans?" I asked Stacy, with my hands underneath me and my head squished to one side.

"Yes," she told me. "You don't want to actually touch your own vagina."

No fucking kidding. That was out of the question. I had enough trouble even *looking* at my own vagina every morning when I pulled on my Mary Lou Retton underwear.

I had finally discovered what most English-speaking people refer to as the "vagina" but what my family referred to as the "coslopus" (kuh-SLOP-us). I wasn't prepared for what kind of ride this little magic muffin was going to

2

take me on, but I reminded myself that we never choose who we fall in love with, and I had no choice when my little hot pocket in a pita took over my life for the good part of the third and fourth grades.

My initial feeling when looking down at my private area was one of disgust. From my earlier self-examinations, the only thing I could deduce was that my private area was similar to a pincushion in structure, but less radiant. You can imagine my feelings of conflict when I watched one of my brother's porn tapes and found out that in a few more years pubic hair would be joining the party. This was obviously horrific news, but after seeing a very special episode of *The Jenny Jones Show* about a pair of Siamese twins separated at age thirty-four, I had made it a point that I would always look for the positive in any situation. Even if that situation involved me having all of my sexual encounters up to the age of thirty with my sister connected to me. For instance, on the upside, I would be able to hide my coslopus's contents under the mound of pubic hair that was right around the corner. Were pubes better than just the pincushion by itself? This topic alone plagued me for a fortnight. Pubic hair or pincushion by itself? It basically came down to six of one, half a dozen of another. I learned an important lesson during my third-grade year: Avoid all direct contact with any part of your body you can hide something in, and stay away from Siamese people—and Siamese cats, for that matter.

Had I known as I walked up the hill to Stacy's house

that night, I was about to embark on one of life's greatest adventures, I would have gotten there forty-five minutes earlier.

"Now," she explained, "just keep rubbing the outside of your pants so that they rub against it. If you keep doing it, you'll get 'the feeling.'"

"Can I have a bolster or something for my head?"

"I don't have any more," she told me. All the other girls had gotten there earlier. I took my *Three's Company* suitcase and placed it under my head for support. After that was drenched, I had no choice but to put my head facedown on the carpet. A lesson I wouldn't need to learn twice.

Two hours and twenty minutes later, I was covered in sweat, with rug burns on my forehead and both cheeks. I was in a marathon with my coslopus, and I couldn't break for more than a minute at a time. Every time my eyes would start to roll to the back of my head and I'd feel the exhaustion, I'd get a little tingle and know there was another boom-boom right around the corner. I kept coming back for more. I couldn't get enough of myself. Who was this girl who had been hiding from me for so long? We were one and the same—soul mates, if you will. The carrot to my clitoris.

Who knew that something I could barely look at could give me such pleasure? Who knew that the little albino pincushion I was carrying around all these years would end up turning into the equivalent of a watermelon Jolly Rancher? How many other women knew about this? And if they did, why did anyone ever get jobs?

After I had completely sweated through my jeans and T-shirt like a rapist, I quickly changed into my *Fantasy Island* pajamas. "Hold on, Tattoo," I said, looking at his face printed on the pocket of my pajama top. "I'm about to show you what real paradise is all about."

I tried every different position I could imagine. I lay on my back and got myself from the front. Then I'd make a backward bridge and get myself from the top. I got on all fours and then took myself from behind, then turned on my side with one leg in the air erect, like a boomerang. Every few minutes I would come up for a couple sips of cherry CapriSun and to wipe the drool off my cheek, and then it was back to business.

I got out my sleeping bag and lay on that for more cushioning. I turned around on my back and kicked both legs out on either side in a split. I tried a scissor kick while simultaneously probing my two forefingers down the inseam of my pajamas and ended up kicking our friend Kim right in the face. "Ow!"

I looked over and realized I had woken Kim up. "How could you sleep at a time like this?" I barked.

"What are you doing?" she asked groggily. "Everyone's asleep."

There was no time for sleep. This was go time, and I wasn't going to let another formative year pass right underneath my nose, *or* my coslopus.

Not only did getting "the feeling" feel borderline amazing, I felt like I was really recruiting some unused muscle tissue. My little eight-year-old thighs were burning, and the arches of my feet were cramping. I'd have to throw my leg out like a kickstand to alleviate the pressure, but I was hesitant to take a break. What if I couldn't get the feeling back? What if this was a onetime deal, like a Saturday at the Chrysler-Plymouth Auto Sale?

This is what my phys-ed teacher meant when she talked about "connecting with your body." This is a fucking connection, all right. Instead of doing pointless stretches and dumb fifty-yard-dash drills, we could've been doing a whole different kind of drill that would've achieved the same goals, fitness-wise. Climbing those ropes with the knots on them took on a whole new meaning. I would lodge my coslopus on top of one of those knots, stick my legs straight out, and start groaning. I hadn't felt eroticism like this since I first laid eyes on a Ms. Pac-Man machine, but even that didn't really compare, because at some point an arcade has to close. *I* was open twenty-four hours a day.

So many thoughts were running through my head, from unicorns to high-speed car chases to why would a woman ever need a man if she could make herself feel so outrageous? Why did she even need to leave the house? Maybe *this* is what stay-at-home moms did all day. Maybe they just sat around and played with themselves while watching *Days of Our Lives*, and then *Another World*, and then *General Hospital*. Why would anyone go to college, when you could just meet a guy, send him to the factory, and spin your baby bean all day? The only warning my mother had given me about too much pleasure was with regard to chocolate. "Life is like a box of chocolates," she told me. "Eat too many and you'll end up with your father's tits."

I didn't know at the time that what I was doing would be considered masturbating, but I definitely knew enough to know that I needed to be somewhat discreet when accommodating myself. My parents had never had the birds-and-the-bees conversation with me, and neither did any of my sisters or brothers. I once asked my father about where babies came from, and he told me that "sometimes Daddy parks his car in Mommy's garage." I had no idea what that could possibly mean, but I never went into the garage again.

The only conversation about a penis I'd ever had was with my next-door neighbor Jason Rothstein. The Rothstein family lived next to us for my whole life, and they had two sons who were good friends with my brothers. My brothers and I were always over at their house until for some reason, one night while playing Tip the Waiter with Jason, he decided to pull his pants down and show me the tip of his penis. I had been sitting Indian style on the floor across from him when this happened, and I was on my feet and out the door before it dawned on me that there should be punishment for this kind of behavior. I turned around, and as he and his penis tip were getting up off the floor, I, in my best law-enforcement impersonation, threw my leg up and kicked him right in his balls. I then did a follow-up with one of my signature back-of-the-head slaps. This has the effect of making you feel not only bad but stupid. It being my first one-on-one penis interaction, I was horrified. Like most unpleasant experiences regarding the penis, the first time is always the worst time.

I went barreling down the Rothsteins' steep driveway, gaining just enough momentum for me to make a sharp right and run straight up my own driveway and through my front door in less than sixty seconds. I stormed into the kitchen, where my parents were eating dinner. "Jason Rothstein just showed me his penis."

"What?" my father asked, looking up from his newspaper.

"His penis?" my mother asked, in a way that made me think this was the first she was hearing of this so-called object.

"Yeah, we were in the middle of playing Tip the Waiter, and then he pulled down his pants and changed the game to Tip of His Penis."

"What did you do?" my father asked me, still holding on to his paper.

"I kicked him in the balls and ran back here."

"Good response," he said, looking back down at whatever article he was reading. "Don't go over there again."

"Thanks for the hot tip, Dad. Shouldn't we press charges or something?"

"Press charges against a penis?"

"Yes."

"Don't you think that would be going a little overboard?"

"No, Dad. I'm eight. Are you familiar with the term 'molester'?"

"He didn't do anything to you, did he?"

"No, Dad, but that's not the point. He's obviously in love with me. He's fifteen, and he's got a crush on an eight-year-old. You don't think there's anything sick about that?"

"Oh, please, Chelsea, your mother and I are ten years apart."

A few minutes later, my sister Sloane came into my room without knocking. "Jason's asked me to take my pants down three times. Don't think you're anything special."

I was in the middle of organizing my sticker collection and was laser focused and therefore more than a little irritated by her intrusion. "He obviously respects me more, Sloane. Any guy who asks to see yours first isn't interested in anything long-term. You've got a lot to learn," I advised her.

"Like you know anything about boys," she told me.

"Oh, really, dipshit? I knew that I wouldn't be going back over to my neighbor's house for seconds and thirds after he told me to pull my pants down. You're a moron."

"He never *told* me to pull my pants down. He *asked* me to, and I declined."

"So then why do you keep going over there?"

"Because they have the new Nintendo and better games."

Sloane was pathetic and I knew it, but I also needed

her to know it. "Let me fill you in on something, Sloane. I'll be married twice before you even go on a date. I'm way more fun to be around. Plus, it's obvious I'm going to have a huge rack. My boobs are going to be way bigger than yours, and I have hips. You have a body like Cathy the cartoon character. Please see yourself out."

The fact that Stacy's sleepover came just a few weeks after this incident was serendipitous to say the least. After getting a glimpse of Jason's penis and accidentally seeing one of my father's balls at the beach the previous summer, I was pretty intent on never having sex with a man. I spoke to my father at length not only about covering his balls but also how, if he was going to insist on wearing sweatpants, he would have to use support briefs or put one or both balls in a Ziploc bag before getting dressed. I was willing to accept either option, which I thought generous considering my hatred of men in sweatpants. "Even Russians have the decency to wear tracksuits!" I howled.

I was the last one to leave Stacy's house the next day and didn't question until much later in life why no one said good-bye to me. I was doing the walk of shame through the woods to my house, wearing my still-damp-from-the-night-before jeans, when I noticed how sore my calves were. What . . . a workout.

I wasn't home for an hour before I needed more. I vacillated between wanting to report a rape and feeling more alive than I ever had in my first three-quarters of a decade on earth. I told my mom I was turning in for the night.

"It's six o'clock, Chelsea."

"I know, but we stayed up really late and I am . . . wiped *out*," I told her, feigning a yawn, and then I pumped my arm the way one would do when signaling an eighteen-wheeler to blow its horn.

I ran upstairs, took off my clothes, and changed into a clean T-shirt and a fresh pair of jeans. As I didn't yet have a lock on my door, I propped myself up against the wall next to my door so that I could avoid anyone walking in and seeing me humping myself.

Talk about elevating your heart rate! I felt as if Popeye's forearms had taken up residence in my calves. This was my first introduction to strength training, and it was unforgettable. If I kept this up, which at that point wasn't even open for discussion, it was clear that, due to the muscular development in my calves I soon would only be able to wear cutoffs.

With this kind of definition, it was inevitable that I would be approached for soccer, softball, and possibly even water polo. The fact that water polo wasn't a sport offered at any school wasn't an issue. After people saw what I was able to bring to the table physically, it would be clear that a team would be started, and probably a league. I began fantasizing about what coaches and recruiters would say to reel me in after I'd fake having interest in athletic pursuits.

"Ms. Handler," one of the humorless, dykey-looking coaches would say upon approach. "May I call you Chelsea?"

I would say no.

"Okay, well, Ms. Handler, calves and muscle development like that at such a young age would be uncategorically preposterous to waste. You were obviously put on this earth to play soccer." I would act coy and maybe guffaw, all the while knowing it wasn't a soccer ball I could handle but a little tiny football hiding right inside my peekachu that I would have all to myself for the rest of my life.

"Ding-dong!" I would say aloud to myself in my bedroom while tapping myself on the shoulder. "Who is it? It's me again!" Round and round and round I went. Life was better than a box of chocolates, and it was certainly better than my father's tits. I look back at that time in my young life with fondness, nostalgia, and a touch of disgust.

It wasn't long before I needed to masturbate all the time. I started coming home from school and watching *Oprah* in our second living room in the back of the house. The heat was hardly ever on in that room, and I discovered through practice that I could get extremely passionate with myself and heated up quickly, so a cold room was a bonus. I found a small oscillating fan in our basement and would place it six inches in front of my head. I would position my ass directly behind the ottoman, so if anyone walked in, all they would see was my feet fishtailing and my head propped up on a pillow. When my mother would walk in wondering why I was spending the better part of my days in an unheated living room with a fan on in the middle of winter, I would tell her I thought I was going through early menopause. When she explained that I would have to hit puberty before experiencing early menopause, I quickly changed my tune and welcomed her theory. "I guess I'm just bursting into womanhood" became my byline.

When my brothers would come home from college, they would always hang out in the second living room, but that didn't stop me. I would sandwich myself in between one end of the sofa and the ottoman, and all they could see was my head pop out so I could check to see if they were watching me and wipe my brow with a beach towel. I sometimes wondered if they had any idea what I was doing, but I had grown so accustomed to sexually assaulting myself whenever necessary that my self-awareness became clouded. It never occurred to me that when I got up from one of these positions, the other people in the room would wonder why I was drenched in sweat with my jeans wedged up to my nipples, my eyes crossed, a severe case of cameltoe, and chapped lips. I didn't care. I had bigger fish to fry.

School was becoming a nuisance. It was nearly impossible to go eight hours without jerking off. I had two options to get me through the day: I could use a ruler under my desk during spelling, because our teacher was always at the front with the big ruler, or I could wait until recess to use one of the metal poles that kept the swing sets upright. I would ride the pole up and down until my neck started spasming; on multiple occasions I ended up head-butting myself into the pole.

One by one, my classmates would dismount from the swings as the bell rang, while I would still be writhing on the pole a half hour later. Eventually a hall guard or teacher would come out and yell, "Chelsea, the bell rang thirty minutes ago!"

"Shut up," I'd moan. "It's coming!"

I found myself carving out windows of time in the day and after school for me to be alone with myself. My desire to blow off birthday parties happened to correspond with a precipitous drop in invitations. I didn't notice that I had fewer friends, and frankly I didn't care. Like any person in a new relationship, I had eyes for only one person, even though the person I had eyes for only had one eye.

As soon as spring came along, bike rides took on a new meaning. I would bike for hours on the weekends, rubbing my coslopus on my banana seat. I would ride up and down our block, passing our neighbor's window with my legs extended out to the sides, avoiding any oncoming traffic at the last minute by detouring into a rain gutter. By the end of the school year, I had flipped my bicycle three times and was wearing two silver caps over the teeth I'd lost during orgasms. The vinyl on my seat had started to wear down, so I decided to tape an eraser to the tip of my seat for multiple climactic sensations. I had a basket on my bike and would run out of the house with homework to fool my mother into thinking I was on a deadline.

"My mind comes alive in the cross breeze," I would tell her.

"How are you able to do your schoolwork while you're riding a bike?"

"It is what it is, Mom. You say tomato, I say banana seat."

I would get so excited on Friday nights, knowing that my peekachu and I would be able to have the whole weekend to ourselves. I always had to watch TV while hooking up with myself, just in case anyone walked into my room, which in hindsight seems a little dissonant. Reruns of *Three's Company* and *Growing Pains* weren't exactly titillating, but I had no idea that what I was doing was titillating, since it didn't involve my father's tits. I didn't need imagery to get my party started. I just needed friction.

I decided to start sampling different clothing options and find out which materials aided what I would later find out were orgasms. One would think that sweats or leggings would be optimal, but one would be mistaken. Too easy. Shorts and skirts were off-limits, as they allowed closer to direct contact, which could result in pole burns or, even worse, me actually touching my own MINI Cooper.

I had graduated to the bed and would lie on my stomach, put the comforter over me to conceal any wrongdoing, and turn my head to the side on the pillow so I could stare straight at my TV. If my neck grew cramped, I would switch to lying on my back with the covers over me. I liked this position because, besides being much less suspicious, it worked different muscle groups.

As with any normal relationship in bloom, we

experienced the highs and lows that go hand in hand with the decision to share your life with someone. We spent the summer of '83 together, which grew more challenging due to the increase in the temperature. There were many times I was tempted to walk away, but I always came back when the sun went down. In hindsight it was easier to stay in the relationship than to jump back into the dating scene. With my invisible friend, Lucy, acting as officiator, my coslopus and I had a commitment ceremony where we vowed to be faithful, even though cheating on me would have been impossible for her, considering she was attached to my groin.

It wasn't until Thanksgiving dinner in fourth grade that I was confronted about my romance. My parents had invited some family friends over, along with my five brothers and sisters. I was still in a honeymoon period with myself and didn't take a Thanksgiving dinner seriously enough to not bring my gentleman caller. I had a wooden soup spoon under the table in between my legs, over my corduroys, pursuing my usual enterprise. After several beads of sweat dripped into my pumpkin soup, my father yelled out in front of the whole table, "Chelsea! Stop what you're doing right now!"

Then my mother chimed in. "Chelsea, that is something you want to do in the privacy of your own room."

My brother Ray took this as his cue to announce, "She does it all the time!"

The idea that what I'd been doing to myself for the

past year and a half had not been a secret by any stretch of the imagination came as a shock to me. I couldn't believe I'd been outed. I was mortified, sabotaged, and, worst of all, forced to spend the rest of elementary school ignoring my lover and her pitiful attempts to reconcile. Once it was established that it was not acceptable behavior, I had no desire to do it. No remorse. No breakup letter. No counseling. Just cold turkey. "Au 'voir," I told my coslopus that night before reading my newest issue of *Highlights* magazine, which I had started subscribing to at the age of three.

I think back with fondness on that year I spent getting to know my hot pocket. While some people and the authorities took issue with it, I considered it reasonable and fair. The way I saw it was, if you looked down and saw a brownie sundae with the works sitting in your lap, day after day after day, eventually you're going to attack it.

After I was found out, I didn't contact my clitoris for years. I deemed it untrustworthy and bizarre. I felt the same way about penises. That's why I gave my first hand job with a sock.

Years later when I moved to Los Angeles and walked in on my roommate masturbating in her bedroom the normal way, naked, I almost vomited. "First of all, ya sicko, you need to put some jeans on," I told her. "Then you need to find yourself a playground."

Chapter Two

When Life Hands You Lemons, Squeeze Them into Your Vodka

Whoever the clueless bastard was who thought up the Cabbage Patch Kid better hope I never see him face-to-face. The invention of this bizarrely appealing doll that came with a birth certificate covered in cabbages and whose muscles had completely atrophied pretty much marked the end of me fitting in with anyone but my cleaning lady. The invention of this doll, combined with my early obsession with masturbating and the ridiculous secondhand clothes I was forced to wear, prevented anyone in the third grade from wanting to be alone with me.

My parents couldn't have been more unreasonable when it came to fads or clothes that weren't purchased at a pharmacy. The first hurdle I can remember having to deal with was Barbie dolls, which were a rite of passage for every kindergartner with a half carafe of dignity. I remember explaining to my mother that I needed a Barbie and I needed one fast. Not a hand-me-down from my sister Sloane, who had given all of her Barbies lesbian haircuts in honor of Jo from *The Facts of Life*. I told her I needed a brand-new one with a decent outfit, something appropriate for Bora-Bora or the Jersey shore. My mother reassured me she'd head right to the store after she dropped me off at school one morning. Not surprisingly, when I returned home later that day on foot, because once again my parents had forgotten they had a daughter, my mother ran down the stairs to show me my new "Barby" with a *y*. Unlike Barbie with her gloss finish, this "Barby" came with a matte finish, three bald spots, and a working vagina.

After the Barbie craze came the Atari craze, which my parents refused to participate in. My father explained to Sloane and me ad nauseam why video games polluted the mind, and if we really wanted to retain some knowledge, we should watch the stock-market channel and try to figure out what all the Dow Jones abbreviations on the ticker stood for. I wanted to tell my father to go fuck himself. If he knew so much about the stock market, why did we have air-conditioning only in our dining room? I didn't understand why he had no interest in seeing his daughter excel socially, or why my parents even bothered to have me when they already had five other children who had put them in the hole. It felt like every day there was another mountain to climb, and I just wanted that mountain to take form on the screen of our television set as an Atari video game called Asteroids.

I remember watching documentaries on African countries where children were starving and getting swarmed by flies. I recall thinking that at least their parents were by their side trying to protect them from the flies and trying to gather them food. My parents were busy living their own lives. If I saw a fly, they would just tell me to get out of the way or sarcastically suggest I call Youth and Family Services. What they didn't know was that I had been in contact with Youth and Family Services several times and was one phone call shy of sealing the deal on my emancipation.

Every time a new trend came along, I died a little inside. By the time third grade rolled around, kids started to get their wits about them, and it didn't take long to realize I was not cutting the mustard. I wasn't even cutting the mayonnaise. I knew that my parents would never fall for what was "hot" on the market. The word "hot" wasn't even in their stream of consciousness. The two of them were about as "hot" and "with it" as cerebral palsy. They had about as much empathy for my situation as I did for the stupid cat they brought home for me one day after I asked for a Smurf.

"You can learn a lot more from a cat than you're going to learn from some blue plastic action figure," my father informed me.

"Oh, for chrissake, Dad, they're not action figures. They're peaceful blue little people. They're from a village. And what am I going to learn from a cat? How to take a dump in a box and then walk back into a room like nothing happened?"

"Chelsea. Watch your goddamned mouth. You talk like a truck driver."

"Well, Dad, it's not like we're poor. Why can't you just buy me what I ask for so I can fit in with everyone else?"

"You are eight years old, and as long as you live in this house, you are under our supervision. Cats can be wonderful animals, and anyway, it will be an outdoor cat."

"It doesn't matter if it's an outdoor cat. It will still take a shadoobie in the backyard and walk right back in the house all bright-eyed and bushy-tailed, like, 'Hey, what'd I miss?' I'll tell you what you missed, you cat, you missed wiping your ass!"

"Chelsea, go to your room until you learn how to communicate like an adult!"

Whenever my father yelled, he would also walk toward you and, more often than not, end with a slap in your face, so I was quick to sidestep the sofa and avoid him by doing a cartwheel straight into my bedroom. Then I peered out of my door for one last comment. "There's a reason you never see anyone's house with a Beware of Cat sign.

Because they're not even worth mentioning." As soon as he attempted to get up from the couch, I slammed the door and hid under my bed.

I used to look at that cat with such disgust. Even dogs have the dignity to go find a private area before dropping a deuce. Only cats think they have nothing to hide and can get away with just a couple of back kicks to alert the area that's about to be unsanitized that it's got something coming its way. And then that's it. They walk right back into the room, sometimes even have the gall to hop onto the sofa and look around like, "Hey, whose turn is it to contribute?" I decided to name the cat Poopsie Woopsie. It was the nicest way to say, "I just took a poop, whoopsie."

I used to stare at the cat and imagine how many Smurfs I could fit into it. Then I thought about painting the cat blue and throwing it in the microwave like a little Shrinky Dink. It would be the Smurf no one had. I had terrible thoughts like these throughout my childhood, and luckily I never acted on most of them. It was a Tourette's of sorts; I knew that the thoughts were bad, but I couldn't stop them from entering my mind. I just wanted some fucking Smurfs. Why did the cat have to take up the same amount of space as fifty Smurfs yet bring absolutely nothing to the table? It would just sleep and sleep for hours, like it had nowhere to be and nothing to do. My sister Sloane loved the cat and would try to trap it under her covers, but Poopsie Woopsie wanted nothing to do with Sloane and craved the lack of attention I gave to it, so we ended up spending most of our time together, with the understanding that there was going to be very little affection. Sloane always accused me of turning Poopsie Woopsie against her, but the truth was, the cat could tell that my sister was "off," and by "off" I mean Mormon.

After a while I just accepted that the cat was always in my room. Poopsie Woopsie had impeccable timing; the only time it would ever scratch my door to get out of my room was right before one of my orgasms. The cat was a dick, and he or she knew it. I don't recall if it was a boy or a girl because I never bothered to ask it.

By the time the Cabbage Patch craze came around, I knew I was screwed. If I couldn't reason with my parents about why it was important for them to buy reputable snacks for my lunches, like Snickers or Reese's Peanut Butter Cups, so that I didn't have to unwrap a single Rite Aid imitation Nut Cluster in front of everyone at my lunch table, I knew that this Cabbage Patch bullshit was going to be the end of me.

One day after school, I walked into our living room, turned off *General Hospital*, and joined my mother on the living-room sofa. She had a half-eaten liverwurst sandwich on her lap, so I quickly threw that out the sliding glass door and watched our dog, Mutley, spring out of his doghouse like a hyena.

"Listen up. We're at a crossroads, and I need your help. Everyone at school is talking about Cabbage Patch Kids, and the word is that Toys 'R' Us is getting a new shipment tomorrow morning. So what I'm going to need from you is to get in line at Toys 'R' Us first thing tomorrow morning and get me one of those dolls. You're gonna need to be there by seven," I told her, excusing myself after settling what I had on my docket.

"Why do I need to go to the store at seven in the morning to get one of these?"

"Because they are selling like crazy, and they will run out. They keep running out all over the country! Don't you watch the news? This is go time. I know which one I want. Do you understand?"

My mom was always more reasonable than my father, but she lacked the determination and perseverance needed for the execution of such a task.

"Of course, sweetie, we can get you a doll, but I really don't see the point of getting there so early. Surely everyone else's parents aren't doing that."

"Yes they are! Everyone's parents are doing it. Mom, this is my childhood. This is the only one I get, and by the end of the week everyone is going to have one of these dolls except me, because you guys are stuck in the Dark Ages. I am trying to make the best out of my circumstances, but you and Dad just keep holding me back. This is just like what happened in nursery school when I had to repeat the year because you guys kept forgetting to take me."

"Nursery school is a waste of time," my mother would tell me when I would try to pull her out of bed. "First grade is where things really start to matter," she'd mumble as she rolled over onto a piece of cheddar cheese. My parents thought it was "too cold" throughout most of winter to get themselves dressed and wait for one of our "automobiles" to warm up. Even though I was only five, it was a safe bet to say that my whole life would be based on doing the exact opposite of what my parents did.

I took to calling our next-door neighbor Mrs. Rothstein. I was too embarrassed to ask her for rides myself, so I'd try to put on a German accent and pretend I was my mother. "Vould you mind taking Shell-sea to school today?" I'd say. "None of ze cars vill start."

Mrs. Rothstein knew it wasn't my mother calling but was impressed by my scholarly ambition and always ended up taking me when my parents faked paralysis.

It wasn't getting an education I was interested in, but more an ardent desire to avoid taking fucking naps in the middle of the day on a godforsaken floor mat. I had no time for sleep in the middle of the day. I wanted action, and naps just reminded me of my parents and the meaningless lives they had carved out for themselves. That wasn't the life I wanted for myself, and I certainly had no plans of becoming a geisha, which would be the only other career choice that would require me to practice sleeping.

"Okay, okay, I'll get the doll, Chelsea. I just wish you weren't so dependent on material things to make you feel like you fit in."

Easy enough for someone who walked around the house

all day in a floor-length skirt hoisted over her boobs with no bra to talk about not fitting in. She didn't want to fit in. That was the difference. I did. I wanted a life for myself, and the life I had in mind didn't involve either of my parents. What she really wanted was to avoid having to put on a bra and some decent shoes that were necessary to tackle the New Jersey winter.

"If this were a Latter-day Saints doll, I'm sure you'd be there with bells on and a nipple ring."

"Chelsea, don't be ridiculous. No one's getting a nipple ring."

"I want the brunette Cabbage Patch with green eyes, one dimple, and no freckles." I had freckles, and I thought they looked like a rash. "She is the one I want. Not a boy one. A girl. Check for the coslopus. Do you copy?"

I had seen a couple of boy ones at school, and they looked like something straight out of a seventies porn video with their Jew Afros. All the other girls had the blond ones with blue or brown eyes, or the brown-haired with blue eyes. I wanted green eyes. I hadn't seen one of those yet but knew they were out there. This was my chance to make my mark and get the same thing every kid craved but also show some originality. For the very first time, I would have everyone ogling something *I* had.

At that moment my sister Sloane walked in and announced she wanted a Cabbage Patch, too. I told her to go take a hike in a fucking lake. There was no way she was going to get in on this action. We'd be lucky if my dad came back from the store with the limb of a Cabbage Patch doll, never mind two complete ones.

"Step off!" I told her. "Go to your room."

"Shut up, you can't tell me to go to my room. Why don't *you* go to *your* room and dry-hump your pillow?"

"Mom!" I wailed.

"Girls," my mother interrupted. "Pipe down."

"You do not need a Cabbage Patch doll," I told Sloane. "You are thirteen. You need to get a grip."

"If Chelsea's going to get one, then I want one."

"Sloane, you are a little old for a Cabbage Patch doll," my mother told her.

"Can we please focus on *my* doll? Did you get the brown hair with green eyes?"

"Chelsea, please write it down for me. It sounds very specific. How many different types are there?"

"Thousands!" I wailed. "I don't want a blonde or anyone with brown eyes. *Green* eyes. They have ones with two dimples, but I just want one dimple. The ones with two dimples look too fake, and the ones without dimples look like Chucky. This is a very precise assignment. No matter what, Mom, please, please do not screw this up. Under no circumstances are you to come home with a redhead."

I knew early on about redheads and how they were prone to melanoma. I wasn't about to invest in a child, only to lose her years later to cancer. Plus, I had a young childhood friend named Farrah Linklater, and her whole family had red hair. Thick, unruly red hair that would inevitably end up in one of the dishes they served at dinner. They were like a tribe, an Indian tribe who took up weapons against other single-hair-colored families. Red hair was always suspicious to me, like something made out of synthetic fibers. I imagined that when redheads slept, their hair wove together like the mangrove trees you find in the Florida Keys that grow underwater. They knew they were a minority, and the more consolidated they became, the greater the danger. The only thing I could imagine more suspicious than a regular redhead was a black redhead, but I knew that whatever company was in charge of Cabbage Patch dolls was not nearly progressive enough to throw that at the marketplace.

Just then my father walked through our front door in his ridiculous rain boots that he wore all year long regardless of the weather. He had three newspapers trapped in his armpit, which I knew meant trouble.

My father believed that he was a Thornton Wilder type of character and never tired of impressing upon us how important it was to read. He would bring three newspapers home every week for me to peruse—the *New York Times*, the *Boston Globe*, because he thought that was a very well-written newspaper, and our local paper, the *Star-Ledger*. Once a week he would expect me to write a report on my favorite current-events story in each paper. As if in the third grade I gave a shitstain about how Reagan was reaching across party lines or, even worse, whatever 7-Eleven they were remodeling in a neighboring town. These weren't exactly hot topics for third-graders. At that point in my life, I was looking to reach across my own party lines, and the clearest way to do that was with one of these god-damned Cabbage Patch dolls, not an op-ed piece in the *New York Times*. It never occurred to my father to maybe put down the paper once in a while and actually get busy looking for a legitimate job that might take him out of the house for more than two hours at a time.

I leaped up from the sofa and announced I felt a bout of diarrhea coming on, which was really the only ailment my father ever took seriously.

"What did she eat?" he asked my mother.

"Cat shit," I said, running out of the room. "The kids at school made me eat cat shit today, because I'm wearing jeans from Sears."

My father believed at the time that reading was the only way for me to succeed in life. "You must not let your mind get weak." He never mentioned anything about not letting your bladder get weak, which turned out to be for-tuitous for him and the hundreds of pairs of pants he's ruined since.

My mother came into my room later to ask how much the dolls were, and when I told her, she told me that my father would not be happy. By this time in my life, I'd had enough of their shenanigans and bargain hunting, and I definitely felt like I had plenty of stored resentment to make a case for myself. I walked into the living room, where my father had parked himself with a corned beef on rye, and stated my case.

"Here's the deal, guys. I can't go on like this. *We* can't go on like this. You two are a joke. I am nine years old, trying to make the best out of a situation that is unlike any of my peers'. I have five older brothers and sisters who seem to have fared better than me, mostly because you birthed them when the two of you had a clue as to how to raise a child. I am competing with people in this neighborhood who have access to swing sets, and in-ground pools I can only dream of, and cars that work the first time you try to start them. This isn't a good foundation for the rest of my life, because I will only end up never feeling like I'm enough or of any worth. I will depend on my looks, which will turn me into a shallow, eating-disorder whore who will end up selling her body just so she can buy herself an eternity ring. Reading the *Boston Globe* is not helping my cause. I can read the *Boston Globe* when I'm twenty. Right now I need to read *Sweet Valley High* and watch *Family Ties* and have sleepovers where we get 'the feeling.' I don't even know what you guys do for a living, which brings me to my next topic: Does either one of you have a job?"

"What's 'the feeling'?" my father asked.

"Don't worry about it," my mother interjected to save me. "It's a game they play with peanut butter."

"That's not the point, Dad. I need a Cabbage Patch doll. They're $49.99, and I need one. *Do you copy?*"

"Yes," he said. "I'll go first thing in the morning. You've

made your case. Now, take all the papers into your room, and in exchange for one of these lettuce dolls I'd like you to review what you think of Reagan's trickle-down theory."

"I can tell you my answer to that before reading anything. If it means that people like us are eventually going to get free Cabbage Patch Kids from wealthier Jews in the neighborhood, I'm telling you right now I'm not willing to wait for that leak. I think we already have enough leaks in this house."

"Would you stop it with the complaining all the time? I told you if you see anything leaking, grab some duct tape and pitch in. Weren't you just talking about an arts-and-crafts class?" he reminded me.

"Fine, Melvin," I told him, grabbing the paper out of his hand. "But it has to be the one with brown hair, green eyes, no freckles, and one dimple. One dimple! I'm going to write it down for you. No redheads!"

"What if that's the only kind left, Chelsea? These dolls sound as if they're selling like hotcakes. We can always get a redhead and Mom can color her hair."

"Their hair is made of yarn, Dad. Okay, this isn't one of your Buick LeSabres that you can just spray-paint another color in the hopes of raising the price an extra hundred and fifty dollars and turning it into a 'classic.' Please get real."

"All right, enough already, we got it. No redheads."

Before I retreated to one of the kitchen drawers to retrieve a stained piece of paper that contained some forgotten grocery list that I had probably authored and wrote down the exact description of the doll being demanded, I told them, "And thank you for acknowledging your misstep in having me."

"Jesus Christ, Sylvia, you'd think she was raising us."

"Yeah, no fucking kidding," I mumbled on my way to the kitchen.

The next day at school was torture mixed with excitement. There was a part of me that was hopeful that my father would in fact hold true to his promise. Like a girl in an abusive relationship who hopes that her boyfriend will suddenly see reason and cease and desist with his attacks, I was cautiously optimistic. It was brutal watching everyone at school carrying their Cabbage Patches around, comparing eye color and dimples, who had bangs, who didn't, the birth certificates with their birth weight and full first, middle, and last names.

Instead of masturbating on the swing set that day, I took my forty minutes of recess to kneel in the woods and pray that my cheap Jewish father would somehow muster the courage to spend fifty dollars on a doll that would be able to provide no income for the family.

When I got home, my father was at the "auction." That was a used-car sort of swap meet for people who made no income from buying and selling used cars. The auction was every Tuesday at a place called Skyline. A more appropriate name would have been Loser Alley. This was the only real work commitment my father had all week long, if you could even call it work. The only other times he left the

house were to show a car he had advertised in the newspaper or to go to the grocery store for his pastrami and
corned beef stock-up.

Being at the auction meant my father wouldn't be home
until seven. My mother kept assuring me he would have
a Cabbage Patch with him when he returned. I sat in the
front living room staring out the bay window at our circu-
lar driveway of cars that belonged in an episode of *Dukes
of Hazzard*.

Finally I decided to start working on my Reagan essay,
which was really quite challenging, since I had a hard time
taking him seriously after my brothers and sisters revealed
to me that he'd previously worked as an actor. What a joke.
My father fancied himself a Republican, which was another
joke. I told my father he didn't make enough money to be
a Republican and decided that would be the focus of my
essay. "Misguided Politics" is what I would call it. I started
off by informing the reader, my father, that in order to
consider yourself a member of any political party you first
needed to register to vote.

From my bedroom I saw lights creep up the corner of our
street, and I almost climaxed. I was so nervous I even picked
up Poopsie Woopsie and started violently petting her.

Sure enough, in my father walked carrying the big
cardboard box the dolls came in, with the plastic covering
on the front. I nearly shit my pants.

"AAAAAAhhhhhh!" I screamed. "Let me see!!!!! Let
me see!" I dropped Poopsie Woopsie on my way down the

steps to our front door and ran over to grab the box out of his hands. It was a real live Cabbage Patch Kid! Another second went by before I realized there was no brown hair. There was no hair at all. His name was Stanley. He was a preemie. And he was black.

I finally acquired the Cabbage Patch I had yearned for, Gretchen, when I stole it from my next-door neighbor Jason Rothstein, who had no business being around young girls in the first place.

Chapter Three

Grey Gardens

My boyfriend and I hadn't been seeing eye to eye for weeks. We had just bought a new condo and seemed to be fighting over every detail of its remodeling. Why he would agree to install an eight-by-eight-foot fish tank and then not fill it with a single dolphin made me want to burn his eyebrows off. I saw a side of him that I had never seen in myself: someone with the energy needed to ask lots of questions, get the answers, and then ask more of the same questions in different, annoying ways.

"Chelsea, if you want to make an aquatic statement like that, why don't we get a small sand or tiger shark?" Ted asked.

"I'm not trying to make a fucking statement, Ted. Dolphins are our friends, and sharks are assholes. Why would I want to buy an animal that could potentially go haywire and eat my ass?"

"I'm just trying to make some alternative suggestions."

"Well, Ted, I think a shark is unreasonable. Why not get an electric eel if we're going to go down that road? Maybe something that can escape from the tank and chase us all around the condo like it was on some sort of vendetta? Didn't you see the fourth installment of *Jaws*, where the shark's granddaughter chased the family all the way to the Bahamas? What would we even name a shark, Ted? Hitler, O.J., Manson?"

"Okay, Chelsea, let's just try to stay focused."

Initially, when my designer told me that some couples break up over the design process, I assumed she meant people who were shallow and materialistic: people who drove Toyota Cressidas but also managed to afford eyelash tinting and Invisalign.

The things we were disagreeing over were so menial and exhausting that I almost immediately lost interest in the whole affair. I'm a girl, but not as much of a girl as my boyfriend, so I decided to fold on almost everything. Except for the dolphin.

When he told me he wanted to take his son to Hawaii for his spring break, I thought it might be a good opportunity for me to stay home and ponder how I got myself into this mess in the first place. Hawaii bores me. There is no nightlife, and whenever I'm there, I wake up at seven. If I wanted to wake up at seven, I'd adopt a black baby.

My boyfriend is similar to a large toddler, the only difference being he doesn't cry when he wakes up. He's very animated and has a lot of energy and wants to exert it all at the same time on a variety of activities, which can be incredibly annoying. Coming from a family that specializes in making plans that will most likely never materialize and then being so exhausted from the prospect of an actual outing that we all have to take a nap doesn't really prepare you for the type of person who gets excited by a tide change. Plus, he's twenty years older than me, which makes his behavior even more suspect.

Needless to say, I was euphoric at the idea of spending a weekend alone in my condo with zero responsibilities. The only plan I had was something involving barbecue sauce at my friend's house Saturday night. I was going to spend all weekend planting a tomato garden in my bathtub.

Friday night I went over to a different friend's house and got back home at around two in the morning. Perfect, I thought. I'll sleep in, get up, go for a run, write all day and maybe into the night, and then, depending on my productivity, maybe even make a field trip to Dunkin' Donuts as a reward.

The next morning I woke up at eight-thirty and couldn't go back to sleep. I was pissed. I knew myself well enough not to get up and start being productive. I was thirty-four now. I was a long way from when I first started drinking at around eighteen, and would wake up the next morning super early with a false sense of energy. Then, two hours later, I'd be exhausted, thinking, Why the fuck am I in a canoe?

I went to grab the remote control and thought if I watched a movie, I'd fall right back asleep.

I called my boyfriend in Hawaii.

"How do you turn on the TV?" I asked.

"Which remote do you have, the Time Warner or DirecTV?" he asked with the excitement he usually reserved for fabric swatches or an episode of *Dancing with the Stars*.

Our house is technologically rigged with gadgets and remotes and settings, all of which I have somewhere between slight and zero interest in. When it comes to math or electronics, I am somewhat more advanced than a six-year-old who's been homeschooled by Levi Johnston.

Ted had tried to show me on several occasions what each button on all three of our remote controls did: which operated TiVo, which one was for the toaster, which one massaged your balls, et cetera. It's true what they say about patience being a virtue; it just happens to be a virtue that I choose not to pursue. Quite honestly, I'd rather just get someone else to turn on the toaster.

The bonus of this little setup is that Ted loves his electronics and happens to have an excessive amount of patience, so as a result he loves to tell me all about each gadget, even though he knows my frustration will most likely end with me throwing one of the remotes against a wall or running it through the dishwasher. Since I am also unable to operate the dishwasher, this option is less frequent as it would have to be coordinated with a visit from our cleaning lady, Maria, who comes only on Tuesdays and Fridays. In Ted's never-ending interest in television, he had also recently installed television screens in every ridiculous oversized appliance or mirror that would allow it. There was a TV screen in the bathroom mirror, one on our treadmill, and one in the microwave door. The last proved to be the most confusing of all, because any time you popped something in the microwave, you didn't know if what you saw inside was a roast beef or Al Roker.

Once he guided me to the movie channels, I found my way more easily. I would have to stay within the selection in front of me for fear of losing my place forever, so my options were somewhat limited, but more numerous than before I placed the call to the island of Maui. The upside of this is that I am open to watching almost any movie ever, especially if there's an overweight child in it. I love anything overweight.

I scrolled down until I hit *Nim's Island*. From the looks of things, I could tell that it was ending soon and *Definitely, Maybe* would be starting in twenty minutes. It was safer to commit to a movie I knew nothing about than to browse around looking for other channels, because having the TV backfire on me and my losing my place altogether was always a threat. I'd rather watch something I didn't care about than screw with the remote and gamble with being lost forever in the sports department. I had already lost a weekend the previous fall to women's basketball finals, when I watched a two-hour profile on a six-foot-six black female player, all the time wondering to myself if she would ever achieve half the success of Kobe Bryant and manage to get an entire line of beef named after her.

The first scene I saw of *Nim's Island* was Abigail Breslin swimming underwater at an inhuman velocity in order to rescue another sea animal who looked a lot like Jodie Foster. Jodie had apparently been thrown from a boat but managed to keep her eyes open and breathe for a ninety-second montage. Obviously they were both playing dolphins. "Too soon," I said loudly enough for both of them to hear, as I jumped out of bed to head into the kitchen.

The sun was blinding when I opened the bedroom door. Not realizing how nice a day it was in the main part of the house was extremely irritating. I grabbed a pair of sunglasses and a visor, looked out the windows, and spotted hundreds of boats coming in and out of the marina.

I pulled all the drapes shut. I wanted to be alone and lie in bed for a long period of time. I didn't need to be reminded that other people were outside swimming through life like Nim and Jodie Foster, making the most of their Saturdays, doing cartwheels and high-fiving each other on Rollerblades. I also didn't need anyone looking in my window and seeing me wearing nothing but a visor with the E! logo, sunglasses, and a bra I'd bought three years ago from Walgreens. At this point it was more like a backpack.

I considered taking an Ambien to knock myself out,

but just like with women's basketball, I hadn't had the best acquaintance with this nighttime drug. The last time I tried it, I woke up early one Sunday morning in the backseat of my car with an empty tank of gas and a Crock-Pot of half-eaten spaghetti in the passenger seat.

I looked down at my thighs and thought it best to head over to the freezer and select a Lean Pocket. I don't know who is responsible for coming up with all the different flavors of Lean Pockets, but whoever you are, you have my blessing. Ted does most of the shopping, and thanks to him I had three different options of breakfast pockets, or I could go straight to a midmorning snack and opt for a ham and Swiss or cheeseburger and light cheddar. "I'll start with breakfast," I told myself. "You have all day." Then I opened up the pantry and grabbed a snack-size bag of Cheetos for dessert. I had made it my business to abstain from Cheetos when in another person's company, primarily due to the aftermath of gas but also because of the bright orange residue, which sticks to your fingers and can be shed only at a Korean spa.

I took my meal back to my bed like my mother had taught me to do, but not without being a lady and ripping off half a paper towel and grabbing a steak knife.

Nim's Island was just ending, with a scene on the beach where Gerard Butler appears to be paddling toward the beach in a dinghy straight out of the Pacific. This is where he finds Nim, his eight-year-old daughter he's left for several weeks alone on an island who's made a new friend in

Jodie Foster. Then they all dance around the beach and start a happy new family like a trifecta of sand assholes. Abigail Breslin is around nine in this movie and, from what I could tell, was turning into a real dick.

Definitely, Maybe was about to start. I put three pillows behind me and one underneath my knees in my tireless attempt to thwart osteoporosis. I went back to the kitchen and ripped off the top of a cucumber to dump in my glass of ice water for the total spa experience. I made sure all doors exposing any sort of light were tightly closed, turned my air-conditioning to a breezy sixty-eight degrees, and grabbed some lavender-scented oil, just to have the option for a self-administered foot massage later if I so desired. I checked to see if my eyeshades were on my nightstand in case I fell into a deep, therapeutic slumber, hopped into bed, and took off my visor.

My trainer, whom I had renamed Wolf Woman, texted me to see if I wanted to work out. After months of clinical observation and serious assessment, I had determined that the former bodybuilder I paid to train me was indeed two parts wolf, one part woman. I kept trying to lure her back into her natural habitat, the forest, to observe her there, but she insisted she lived down the street in the Marina. Working out with her was never easy; even if I faked sick, she had little sympathy and was fond of saying, "Your body can do anything for forty-five seconds."

I texted her back. "No."

If I had gone to the theater to see *Definitely, Maybe,* I would never have reacted the way I did watching it in bed. I didn't want it to end, and I couldn't figure out which girl he was going to wind up with. I wanted him with everyone. It was like watching the Olympics and rooting for the United States, but then seeing one of the Up Close and Personal stories about some Russian named Oksana and thinking, Oh, fuck it, just give her the medal. If our American loses, at least she doesn't have to go home to that Russian coach of hers who is probably going to make her live outside the Kremlin in a forty-foot snowdrift until she learns how to dismount without kicking herself in the face.

I was bawling by the time the movie ended, and not in a normal way. It was more like heaving. Heavy, loud groaning, drool coming out of my mouth and nose—not very different from the afternoon I lost my virginity to our neighborhood Santa Claus. I had fallen in love with Abigail Breslin. I hated myself for doubting her in *Nim's Island*. I wanted to call her and apologize but pointed out to myself that we had never met. So I made a mental note to make amends if I ever ran into her at a Chuck E. Cheese or Stride Rite. *I love Abigail Breslin,* I scribbled on the E! notepad next to my bed as a reminder.

It was time for another Lean Pocket. Even though I'm leery of any food item that is not an actual burger but claims to have a burger in it, I knew that these weren't normal circumstances, and I opted for the cheeseburger Lean Pocket. I thought about taking a look outside but didn't want to upset myself further with the sunlight. "It's best to get back to your area," I said with a little disdain, and then noticed a houseplant that needed a trim. So I backtracked to the kitchen to grab my kitchen shears and went and cut the plant some bangs.

Four hours and two Lean Pockets later, I was immersed in the movie version of *Sex and the City*. "Not prepared" is an understatement. I had to pause the movie several times during the wedding to gain control of myself. Not only was watching that kind of rejection heart-wrenching, but my face had become so swollen from crying that I could barely see out of my eyes. I also had a modicum of concern that if my tear ducts didn't get a rest, there was a risk of reversing my recent LASIK surgery. I hadn't cried like this since *Norbit*.

Tissues surrounded me in my bed, along with plates covered in Lean Pocket crusts, because I had eaten only the insides. It dawned on me right there and then, propped up in my bed wearing nothing but my bra and underwear, that I had spent the better part of my day hysterically crying while eating out Lean Pockets.

There were spilled glasses of Diet Canada Dry ginger ale strewn next to my bed that I hadn't even attempted to clean up, leaving the carpet with the same texture it would have if the Octomom's water had broken.

I nearly jumped out of my skin when my landline rang.

I had heard it ring before but was unsure who was calling or how to answer the phone. I looked at it, looked at my BlackBerry, then decided to go to the kitchen and see if the phone in there was any more user-friendly.

I ran out of the bedroom, but in my path was a fork that I vaguely remember hearing fall from one of my plates earlier. In order to avoid stepping directly onto its tines, I maneuvered myself to land directly into the wall. I fall on a pretty regular basis, so I was able to recover quickly enough to yell, "Chelsea, what the fuck is wrong with you? Get your shit together!" Then I got up to make myself a Bloody Mary. My BlackBerry started ringing, and I could see on the screen that it was Ted calling.

"Chunk?" I asked when he answered the phone.

"What's wrong, Chunk?" he asked.

"I just fell and hit my head."

"Are you okay?"

"Not really. I'm watching *Sex and the City: The Movie!*" I sobbed into the phone.

"Oh. I'm sorry."

"I'm so upset," I managed to get out between wails. "P-p-please t-t-tell me y-y-you would never leave me at the altar if we got married."

"But you don't even want to get married," he reminded me.

"Who?"

"When?"

"I said, p-promise me-e-e-e-e that you will never

humiliate me in public, and you'll n-n-n-ever do anything that will make me break up with you."

"I would never do that to you. You'll probably do it to me, but I would never do it to you."

"That's sweet, Chunk. Thank you. I have to go now."

"Honey, maybe you should get up and go for a run or go out. You sound awful. You can't just watch movies all day. Is it nice out?"

"No. There are forty-mile-an-hour winds and it's hailing, Ted."

"Well, it can't be *hailing.*"

"You don't know what's going on here. This isn't some walk in the park like Hawaii, okay? I am deep in the trenches of Southern California."

"Okay, well, why don't you call Hannah or Sarah and go see one of your girlfriends. Are you getting any writing done?"

"I have to go," I said. "I need to learn how to answer the phone."

"You just have to push 'talk.' We've been through this several times. You know this. The whole point of you not coming to Hawaii was so that you would write your book. Please get some work done."

"No, the whole point of you going to Hawaii without me was that you were being so irrational about buying the dolphin."

He groaned. "Enough already. We cannot get a dolphin. I have looked into it, and a single-family house is not big enough to have a dolphin. You were on the speaker-phone when we talked to the Humane Society, Chelsea. And if you remember correctly, their suggestion was that you don't get any pets, period."

I decided to ignore this comment and pressed forward. "Why can't we just get a baby dolphin and I'll smoke a bunch of pot around it so it doesn't grow?"

"Is this conversation over, or are we still talking?"

"No one in the building has to know. We can bring it up through the balcony outside."

"Chelsea, we can't get a dolphin. This isn't an aquarium, and there is no way to hide transporting a dolphin through our balcony. This isn't a private residence. It's a condominium. There are people everywhere. If you know a dolphin dealer who can get a little-person dolphin, then I will do everything in my power to get you one, but my fear is that it will continually just head-butt itself into the front of the fish tank. There is a limit to how big the fish tank can be, and condo living is no life for a dolphin. I told you I can get you a tiger shark. That's legal."

"Fine, you want to get that shark, we'll get that shark. Oh, I'm going to get that shark all right. I'm going to sit in front of the fish tank and give it the finger all day long while I watch it head-butt itself."

I threw my BlackBerry against the wall.

"This is what Ted had intended all along," I said to one of the knives lying on the counter. "To render me completely useless. To have me be dependent on him for everything, so if I ever broke free, I would be forced to return if I wanted to watch TV or preheat an oven again."

What a sham. I looked at the sun desperately trying to creep in from outside, and I felt awful. Why couldn't it just start raining so I would stop feeling so guilty about lying around in my bra and underwear in an environment that would surely be awarded an F by the Health Department?

While I was pouring myself a vodka and Clamato juice, I briefly considered going for a run, and instead I went into my bathroom to get a Vicodin I had left over from the batch I was given after my vaginal-rejuvenation surgery. Before long I drifted into a very relaxing siesta.

When you roll over in bed in the morning and hit a plate with the side of your head, you know things have gotten carried away. When you toss that plate on the floor, roll back over, and fall asleep again, you've hit another dimension. When you look at the clock and realize it's not morning but still the day before, you're either in Australia or you've gone into another dimension that isn't easy to get out of. It takes a discipline that is common only among Cheesecake Factory managers and people who maintain a weight over 350 pounds.

Our landline rang again, and this time I pressed "talk."

"Caller, go ahead."

"Did I wake you?"

"No."

"Did you go for a run?"

50

"Yes."

"Are you writing?"

"Who is this?"

"It's Ted."

"Caller, who are you calling for?"

"The building Realtor wants to show our place tomorrow."

"Negative."

"Because you don't want to clean it or because you want to just lie around all day in your bra?"

"I don't want to clean *and* I want to lie around in my bra, plus I've sustained an injury. Tomorrow's Sunday. Who knows when I'll wake up? It could be noon, it could be four."

"Okay, I can cancel the showing, but then they'll want to come Monday. So should I have Maria come Monday morning, or do you think you'll be able to clean up yourself?"

"I think you should call Maria."

After we hung up, I looked at the clock. Eight P.M. Perfect movie starting time. I scrolled down and saw *Sex and the City* starting again at eight. I could have climaxed right there and then. I walked into my bathroom and saw a soup spoon on the scale and, next to a box of tissues, a cheeseburger ball half on a plate and half on the countertop. I couldn't believe that a tiny little cheeseburger was big enough to split into two on two different surfaces. Those Lean Pockets are full of scientific surprises. I didn't know what was happening to me, but I couldn't fight it. I had to go with my creator.

The fact that *Sex and the City: The Movie* had come out a year before and I'd had less than no desire to see it yet was about to buckle myself in for a second showing in less than twelve hours meant that all proverbial ducks were not in a row. They weren't even ducks. They were seagulls. Dirty seagulls.

I hated Big. I hated everything about him and this story line. First of all, it didn't make any sense that he was getting out of the car to tell her he would marry her and never once said that when she's throwing the flowers at him. I wanted Big dead. I wanted to take the fork that was sitting in my bathroom and stab him in the eyes, right where he has those big puffy circles under them. Stupid-ass shitstain motherfucker. Then Carrie wastes all of her energy being mad at Miranda when the real problem was and always will be Charlotte. Forget what Miranda told Big about getting married. How about being mad at Charlotte for being so stupid? The only decent thing Charlotte's ever done on the show or in the movie is shit her pants, and that does not make up for years of Type 1 retardation.

My friend Sarah called me at around seven-thirty to ask me what time I wanted to go to our friend's barbecue. "Not happening," I told her. "Shit's really hit the fan over here big-time."

"Are you crying?"

"Yes. Have you seen *Sex and the City*?"

"Really, Chelsea?"

"Yes! Really! You were left at the altar, Sarah. Hello! Have some compassion for Sarah Jessica Parker." (See *Are You There, Vodka? It's Me, Chelsea.*)

"So you're going to stay in bed on a Saturday night crying? Is that your game plan?"

"That's my plan, but it ain't no game, girl."

"Have fun. Call me tomorrow if we're all doing happy hour."

"I'll be there for happy hour." I hung up the phone.

My Bloody Mary from earlier had evaporated, so I went to make myself another one and was glad to see the sun had gone down. "Thank God."

As I was stirring my drink, I asked the Clamato juice container, "What is Clamato juice exactly? It sounds like a yeast infection."

After reviewing the label and coming upon the words "clam juice," then spitting out my drink, I moved on to my next drink of choice when resting. A scotch neat with a splash of Crystal Light Hawaiian Punch.

Back in the bedroom, I pressed "play" on the remote, and in doing so felt like I was finally taking control of the situation. Now the girls were in Mexico, and Sarah Jessica Parker was listless and slept and didn't eat. Conversely, I was in Marina del Rey, in my bed, crying into my scotch. I wished Sarah Jessica Parker and I could be in bed together so I could roll over, brush her cheek, and assure her that everything would be okay. Then I remembered that having a guest visit would require me to tidy up. And I was back to being okay without company.

I fell asleep again toward the end of the movie, so I've now seen the movie twice and never seen the ending. I know that Sarah Jessica Parker and Big get back together, but I don't approve of it, and I won't endorse it. The more interesting news is that I woke up the next morning, got out of bed, took a look around my condo, and got right back into bed.

Another sunrise, another movie marathon. The next morning I worked my way up to Lifetime, but after two commercial breaks I was back to the Starz networks. There's nothing more annoying than infomercials when you can't find your wallet.

After viewing *Reservation Road*, *Revolutionary Road*, and one episode of *Real Housewives of Orange County*, I went online to shop for a handgun with the letter *R* on the barrel.

Sarah called me at around 3:00 P.M. on Sunday, and I burst into tears.

"Chelsea," she said, "you sound like a real asshole. Get your ass out of bed and get in the shower."

"I know! I want to, but I can't. You should see this place. I don't even know how to begin cleaning."

"Don't clean anything. You don't even know how to clean. You're a hot mess."

"I can't go out. *Grey Gardens* is on later, and I need to hear Drew Barrymore's accent."

"Chelsea, you are *Grey Gardens*!"

It dawned on me that she was indeed correct. "Too soon, Sarah. Too soon."

"Just TiVo it."

"What do you think, I live inside a Best Buy?"

"Well, I blame Ted for that. You're practically crippled. I'm surprised you can even answer the phone."

"That's what I keep saying!"

"To Ted?"

"No, to myself."

"Exactly."

"You are supposed to be a grown-up. You have your own television show."

"But it's on E!"

"I know, but you still have a whole staff that is depending on you."

"To go to happy hour?"

"To stay somewhat sane."

"Well, I don't know what to tell you."

"Yeah, so get your shit together. Your shit is *not* together."

"Okay."

"Do you even know how to use the shower?"

"Sometimes." I hung up, took off my bra and underwear, threw them both in the garbage, and got my shit together. I then gave myself a full-body examination, to eliminate the threat of adult-onset bedsores. "All clear!"

After my shower I felt like I had a new lease on life. I knew if I really stayed focused and applied myself, I could actually TiVo *Grey Gardens* later that night. I walked to my car with a little extra bounce in my step and also a little limp, glad I was able to handle some sort of electronics without anyone else's assistance. I now have a season pass to *Grey's Anatomy*.

Chapter Four

Dudley

Every once in a while, I like to send out an all-staff e-mail to find out who the dumbest people working on my show are. The e-mail below is something I asked my assistant to devise based on the fact that we still had a doctor's table for a skit we did on the show called "Dr. Lately." Since production had paid to rent the table and we still had it for a few days, I thought it made perfect sense to get our money's worth and see how many people would believe that a gynecologist was coming in to perform a couple of Pap smears. Here is what Eva sent out to the staff:

Hi there,

   Dr. Clara, MD, will be here on **Tuesday, April 14th from 4:30—6:30pm.** She is available for individual concentration and will be setting up 20—30 minute appointments on stage 2. Dr. Clara is dedicated to providing outstanding care for patients needing pap smears, adolescent medicine, gynecology, infertility, high-risk obstetrics, STD testing and questions relating to male/female health overall. Space is limited so please email me if you would like to schedule an appointment. She will also be providing the appropriate garments for any examinations. Prices and co-pay vary depending on insurance and for more information on Dr. Clara, MD, and her practice, visit: West Los Angeles Women's Care.com.
   Thanks!!

I had Eva CC my boyfriend, Ted, on the e-mail so that he could be aware of how I was spending my day, especially since he also happens to be the CEO of the network that my show is on. Ted's office is in a different building from ours, so we are essentially unsupervised and generally unproductive. Ted, instead of realizing that this was obviously a joke, responded with this e-mail to Eva:

   Don't say anything yet to CH but having outside Dr in is a problem as outlined

below. I'm going to try to help here but at
the very least, the dr is going to have to
sign a letter indemnifying us.

Generally speaking, this is something
we would suggest we avoid and not do on
our premises...but it also seems as if
the wheels have already been put in motion
so we need to consider how to handle that
as well...

Below is the e-mail Ted received from his legal team
later that day, which he forwarded to Eva:

Here are two preliminary concerns.
There may be an expressed or implied
endorsement of this particular physician
by us taking such an active role in setting her appointments and allowing her to
conduct those appointments on premises,
most specifically, pap smears. If the company is perceived as endorsing this physician, do we take on the liability for
anything this physician does (including
a misdiagnosis?). Second concern is that
if there is any medical treatment actually taking place on our premises, are
we covered for that from an insurance
perspective.

> I am checking on these specifically with
> outside counsel and will get back to you
> soon. I can tell you most definitely, that
> any fertility treatments raise a red flag.

As soon as I finished reading the e-mail, I picked up the phone and called Ted. "Do you really think that I'm going to have girls in our office go down to Stage 2 on their lunch break for a quick vagina assessment?"

"Chelsea."

"Ted."

"Chelsea."

"Ted."

"Jesus, Chelsea."

He put his phone down and yelled, "It's a joke. There's no gynecologist. It's Chelsea being an asshole. Again."

"Ted," I said, "did you even read that e-mail that Eva sent? It said the doctor would be available for male/female health-related questions. What gynecologist services men? Either you're a gynecologist or you aren't. You're not a man doctor for women."

"How would I know that?"

"Because you're a man! Have *you* ever been to a gynecologist?"

"I can't believe I fall for this shit."

"I thought I was being nice by including you in the joke, and now the joke is on you. Not the two girls on staff who have already booked their appointments."

"Oh, my God."

"I know."

"Are you going to film it?"

"I hadn't gotten that far, because there was a little bump in the road named Ted."

"Chelsea, I don't have time for this shit. Now I have to go clear this up."

"Ted, the e-mail also said 'individual *concentration.*' It's 'consultation.' What the hell is an individual concentration?"

"Well, I don't know what you girls do in your appointments, Chelsea. That cost us money. You're paying the legal fees. We had to hire outside counsel."

"Yes, I know. That's why I'm calling. I assumed you would know that I wouldn't be doling out fertility treatments on a fake doctor's table at the studio."

"That *is* something you would do!"

"Really?"

"Yes, you're fucking crazy, and you *would* do something like that, and you're paying the legal bills."

"I'll be happy to."

"Good, we'll send you the bill."

"Good. I'd like to frame it and put it in my office."

In true Ted form, he was not in on the joke, which is basically the foundation of our relationship. No matter how much time goes by, I am still able to make him believe stories that no one who has completed high school would believe. On separate occasions I've convinced him that I paid sixteen thousand dollars for a pair of sunglasses, that I donated ten thousand dollars to a charity that helps prevent pit bulls from being forced to wear rhinestone collars, and that a pair of my shoes came with two Swiss Army knives under the soles. The jokes are never well-thought-out plans, more like happy accidents that just pop into my head when I look out the window. That is exactly what happened a few weeks later when Dudley came into our life.

My agents at the time wanted to throw a little congratulatory party celebrating a new deal I had signed. One of them was named John, and he was a rather unusually muscular gay man who lived with an even more unusually muscular gayer man and shared with him an English bulldog named Dudley.

Their house was in the Hollywood Hills and was decorated the exact way you would expect a couple of gay bear millionaires living in the Hollywood Hills to decorate: very masculine, very expensive, and a lot of lubrication.

The house was filled with beautiful art and had a very modern but luxuriously comfy feel. Like a resort. A resort with a prison shower the size of a mosh pit and enough waterfalls for a stranger to slip into another stranger's asshole without a moment's notice. In other words, the kind of spa two gay bears from the Hollywood Hills would like to run.

There were only about nine of us at the little soiree: Ted, two of my agents (John, Claire), my attorney (Jake), my partner (Tom) and his wife (Beth), and Eva, my assistant. I planted myself on the sofa and was talking to Beth and Eva when Dudley sauntered over with his ass in the air, the way only an English bulldog can do.

Dudley was a dick from the word go. He was sniffing around the hors d'oeuvres while simultaneously licking my uncovered leg, so I immediately gave him a fried ravioli. The setback occurred when Dudley thought the fried ravioli was accompanied by the black cocktail napkin it was on, both of which he demolished with little or no struggle from me.

I did make a moderate attempt to save the napkin, but after one overly aggressive tug from Dudley I decided it would make less of a scene if I just gave the napkin to him rather than get down on my knees and wrestle a bulldog. I felt I had maybe made the wrong decision when I looked at Eva, who was staring at the dog, horrified, as the last corner of the napkin disappeared.

"I think we should tell them that their dog just swallowed a napkin," she said, getting up.

I pulled her down to her seat. "No. It's fine. I give napkins to dogs all the time."

Ted walked over to us just as Dudley was ready for more, and I told him what happened. "Oh, he'll be fine," he said. "It's just a napkin."

"It was a four-ply napkin," Eva told him.

"Okay, cool it," I told her, glaring. "It's fine. I didn't

know I had hired a vet," I mumbled loudly enough for her to hear.

"Those dogs can eat anything," Ted said, dragging me by my arm. "Come on, Chelsea. I found another waterfall."

Dudley, of course, was hot on my tail from then on, knowing he had found an ally. "I hope the dog doesn't throw up. At least while we're here," I told Ted as he pulled me outside into a scene out of a Costa Rican bathhouse, but classier.

"We have to get the name of their designer," he exclaimed with a little too much excitement. "This guy is a genius. You can put waterfalls wherever you want."

"Ted, we live in a condo. This compound is more along the lines of an anal jungle. We can't just rip out our roof and stare at the moon. I can find out where we can get those little glow-in-the-dark stars and glue them to the ceiling. Then you can go off."

"Well, we can think of something. This is amazing! What is that smell?"

"It's Dudley," I lied. "It's the napkin."

Actually I had farted, but I sensed an opening in my path, and, not yet knowing in which direction it was headed, I had to leave all options open.

"Is it okay to give a dog shellfish?" I asked.

"Is that what you gave him?"

"Yeah. That crab thing they were passing around."

"I don't know, but don't give him any more. I don't think dogs can eat crab," he said, grimacing at Dudley.

"Come to the bathroom. I want to show you this bidet I want us to get."

"I've seen three bidets in fifteen minutes. I'm good."

"God, it reeks. What the hell kind of napkin was that?"

"The crab was wrapped in butter lettuce. Maybe that's it."

"Oooh, that sounds good. I'm gonna go grab one."

On the way home that night, I mentioned Dudley once more in the car and then let it go. I had to figure out my game plan of where I was going to take this little doozy of a story.

"I can still smell Dudley's farts," Ted declared as we descended a hill so steep that the only safe form of transportation would have been a rickshaw.

"It's not Dudley anymore. It's me."

"Was it you the whole time?"

"Yes."

"Maybe *you're* allergic to shellfish."

In the car on the way to work the next morning, I heard my phone ring and saw that it was Ted. I picked up and started wailing. "John's assistant just called. The dog died after we left last night."

"No!"

"Yes!" I heaved into my steering wheel, which I mistakenly believed held my speaker.

"Oh, my God, you're kidding me, right?"

"Do I sound like I'm kidding, Ted? I haven't spoken to

him yet, but Eva just called me and told me his assistant called. She's calling everyone at the party."

"Oh, my God! Oh, my God! Do you think it was the napkin?"

"It had to have been. Or the shellfish," I reminded him.

"Oh, my God! Do not tell anyone that you gave him the napkin *or* the shellfish. Who else was there when you gave it to him?" he demanded.

"It was just Eva and Beth."

"Okay, just don't tell anyone else that was there. Do not tell anyone, Chelsea. Do you understand me?"

"I don't feel comfortable asking Eva to lie for me if I killed a dog."

"Did she sign her confidentiality agreement?"

"Yes, but she didn't see what I fed Dudley. She just saw the tail end of him eating the napkin. I'll say it was one of those raviolis."

"Okay."

I felt a new wave of fake tears ready to make their way through the phone just in time for me to explode, "I'm a murderer, Ted! I'm a murderer. A dog murderer! I'm just like Phil Spector minus the music career."

"No, Chelsea, you need to get ahold of yourself. You are not a murderer! This was an accidental dog homicide!"

"What if they find out?"

"No one's going to find out anything. Let me make a few calls. I'll call John to give my condolences and feel around to find out if he suspects anything. Stay strong.

You did nothing wrong. This was an accident. Chelsea. . . .
I love you."

"Thanks," I muttered as meekly as possible, and then
added, "His assistant said they were doing an autopsy."

"What?!"

"An autopsy."

"The dog is fucking ten years old! They said last night
they gave him open-heart surgery two months ago."

"I know. That means they think something fishy happened last night. They're going to find out. I can't believe I
killed someone's dog." We hung up the phone, and I spent
the rest of my ride into work craning my head around trying to find out where exactly the speakerphone in my car
was located. Ted's voice had sounded like it was coming
straight out of the sky.

I had an extra bounce in my step walking into the office
that day and headed straight into Tom's office, where he
was sitting with Brad, one of the writers on my show.

"What did you think about that dog Dudley last night?"
I asked Tom as I sat down on the sofa opposite Brad.

"I'll tell you what I thought of Dudley," Tom said, plac-
ing his morning coffee on his desk. "I believe Dudley is
what two bears can produce when they fall madly, deeply
in love under a waterfall. A cub in the shape of a bulldog
that goes by the name of Dudley."

"I thought that dog looked like he could take a punch
in the face. And I wanted to punch him, because he didn't
stop farting all night."

"That was you, and you're a fool if you think everybody at that party didn't know it."

"That may be true, but that's not what I'm here to discuss. Let me tell you a little story about Dudley. Last night I fed him a ravioli, and he ate the whole napkin with it. For Ted's benefit I later changed the ravioli to one of those crab appetizers. I spoke to Ted earlier this morning and told him that Dudley passed away last night and they're doing an autopsy today at three."

Anyone who has seen Brad on the show knows how ridiculous-looking he is, but to see him when his face turns bright red and he is unable to control his heart-attack-like fits of hysteria is worth playing any practical joke on anyone. He immediately starts contorting his body and grabbing his head, and his face turns into the exact color of his ridiculous orange hair. Basically the same way a person would react during an earthquake, minus the laughter. "How can he believe you?" he bellowed as he started writhing on the couch. "How can he believe anything you say anymore? A dog autopsy?! Who the hell gets a dog autopsy?!"

While Brad was going into what anyone walking by the office would perceive to be seizures, Tom was as cool as a cucumber.

"This is excellent work, Chelsea. I like what you've done here."

"You have to call him on speakerphone and let us listen!" Brad sobbed.

"Cool your heels, Tinker Bell," Tom told him. "This

has to be thought out very carefully. You need to call all the other people that were there last night and tell them the deal. There's a lot of potential here. What's your weekend looking like?"

"Wide open."

"Well, why don't we stage a little dog funeral somewhere and have our little producer, Mr. Johnny Kansas, film the whole episode. You're on *Leno* Tuesday night. You know how much Ted likes to be on television."

This was true. As much as he pretends he hates it, Ted loves to be talked about or displayed on television.

"Johnny!" Tom yelled.

Johnny walked in, and Tom asked him what his plans were for this weekend.

"I've got a christening on Sunday," he told us. "I'm free Saturday."

"Then Saturday it is. Where can we have the funeral?" Tom asked me.

"Well, it would have to be somewhere on our side of town, because there's no way I'm going to drive forty-five minutes for a fake funeral. How about the Santa Monica Pier? We can say we're spreading Dudley's ashes because he wanted to be cremated."

"The Santa Monica Pier!" Brad was now slamming his head on the arm of the sofa. "I can't take it! I can't take it! Dog ashes at the Santa Monica Pier!"

"Brad, pull yourself together, you fucking idiot. This is business," Tom told him.

"Okay, okay, okay, wait! You have to do the funeral after five so I can come."

"No, you can't come. You'll give it away before he even finds out," I admonished him.

"No! I have to be there."

"Brad is not coming," Johnny said, looking at him in disgust. "He'll ruin everything."

"Brad, you're not coming," I told him again. "But I will call Ted on speakerphone to tell him about the funeral, and you can listen."

"Not on my watch," Johnny said as he walked out. "I will not be a party to this other than videotaping the funeral."

"Hi, sweetie," Ted said in his very melodramatic way when he picked up the phone.

"They're having a funeral on Saturday at the Santa Monica Pier."

Brad jumped off the sofa and buried himself under Tom's desk, which had been vacated when Tom stood to shut the door.

"A funeral? I just got off with John, and he didn't say anything about a funeral."

"You just got off with John?" I asked, thinking I was screwed because I hadn't even spoken to John yet. "And?"

"And he sounded awful. I don't think he suspects anything. He just sounded terrible."

I looked over at Tom, who was standing by the door rubbing his goatee, and his eyes widened.

"Well, did he say anything about what might have caused it?"

"No, he says they just had open-heart surgery on the dog a few months ago, so he doesn't understand what happened."

The amount of fluid that you could hear coming out of Brad's body was unsettling. Luckily, the desk muffled his fits of laughter enough for Ted not to hear. I walked behind the desk and kicked him.

"He didn't say anything about a funeral, Chelsea. I don't think we have to go."

"No, his assistant is e-mailing everyone at the party. They want everyone who was there when he left the world to be there when he enters the ocean."

That was the only line I actually had trouble delivering with a straight face, and I fumbled a little but made a quick recovery. "It's Saturday."

"Saturday?"

"Yeah."

"Oh, my God. I have to go to a dog funeral on a Saturday?"

"It's at the Santa Monica Pier."

"Well, at least that's not too far."

This was just like Ted, to have a problem with the event as a whole but not take issue with the idea that the dog's ashes were basically being spread off a circus fairground into the Pacific Ocean.

By now the desk was vibrating, and I knew that Brad

wouldn't be able to hold out much longer, so I ended the conversation with a final sniffle. "I'll call you later," I said, then hung up the phone.

"Did you tell John that you were faking his dog's death?" Tom asked.

"No, but he's familiar with the inner workings of this office, so he must have put two and two together."

"Pretty impressive work on John's behalf. I didn't know he had it in him. I think your next move is to have Eva call John's assistant and have her send out an e-mail asking everyone at the party if they saw Dudley eat any of the hors d'oeuvres at the party. And make sure you e-mail Claire and Jake just in case Ted starts calling the whole town."

"Exactly," I replied while looking over at Brad, whose face had turned two shades darker than a lobster.

"After that little desk performance, you are definitely not going to the pier," Tom told him.

"Pleeeeeease?"

I walked over to Eva's desk to give her instructions on the next phase of Operation Dudley Is Dead.

The next e-mail was sent by Eva a few minutes later:

```
Hey guys. Did any of you see Dudley
ingest or eat anything last night that
maybe he shouldn't have? The animal doc-
tor that is doing the autopsy asked John's
assistant to find out. It's a little awkward
so she asked me if I could help.
```

Before I even finished reading the e-mail, my phone rang. "Did you get the e-mail?" Ted asked me.

"Yes. They know it's me."

"No, they do not!"

"They're gonna find out when they do the autopsy. They're gonna find the crab right next to that black napkin in Dudley's belly."

"Yes, but they aren't going to know who did it."

"I have to come forward."

"No, Chelsea! We don't even know if the dog is allergic to shellfish. It could have been something else."

"*Was* allergic to shellfish. Dudley is dead, Ted."

"We don't know that it was the shellfish. It could've been anything. Just wait until we get the autopsy results."

I took a deep, loud, dramatic breath.

"Chelsea," he said in the voice that a grief counselor would use with a patient attempting to do bodily harm to herself. "I have to go into a meeting now. Please don't talk to or call anyone who was at the party. Did you tell Tom?"

"Yes."

"Anyone else?"

"Brad."

"Why did you tell Brad?"

"Because he saw me crying."

"Oh, honey. You poor thing. Sweetie, you have to remember, this was an accident. The dog could have had another heart attack. We don't know it was the crab. It might just have been his time."

73

"I'm fine. I have to go, Ted. This is all too much."

A little later Eva walked into my office to tell me that Ted had called her and made it very clear to her that she saw nothing unusual at last night's party. "He also said that you were in a very fragile state and that I should keep an eye on you." Eva told me all this with a straight face and then turned on her heel and laughed all the way back to her desk. I was impressed with this side of her and her skill set in dealing with an unexpected dog homicide.

Luckily for me it was Friday. The spreading of the ashes would be Saturday, so I would have to go through with this charade for only one night and a morning.

Needless to say I had a terrific day planning the next day's events. I hadn't been this charged up since the presidential inauguration. On my way home from the show that evening, my attorney Jake called.

"Chelsea. I was on the phone with Ted trying for forty minutes to figure out who fed the dog what. He was trying to protect you and convince me you had nothing to do with it. This is so fucking stupid. I kept having to put the phone on mute. Are you really going to take the CEO of a cable company to a dog funeral?"

"Yes, it's at the pier. Would you like to come?"

"Yes, but I have my kid's soccer game tomorrow. Can't we do it Sunday? How can he believe this?"

"Johnny is filming it, and he has a christening on Sunday. Your loss."

"Shit. I really want to see this."

"Well, unless Ted hits me, I'll probably show it on *Leno* Tuesday night."

"You should tell Ted that John's hiring a pet detective to put on the case."

"I don't have time for shenanigans," I told Jake, and hung up.

When I got home, I jumped on the treadmill. As soon as Ted walked in, I texted Eva to send the follow-up e-mail we had coordinated earlier:

```
Hi guys. John's assistant just told me
confidentially that the autopsy revealed
that Dudley was allergic to shellfish and
that seems to be the culprit. Chelsea, if
I recall correctly that is not what you
gave him. I'm pretty sure it was one of
those raviolis. Poor guy!
```

I liked Eva. I liked her a lot.

Our treadmill is on our balcony, and Ted was standing in front of it talking to me when he read the e-mail.

"Oh, dear Lord. I knew it."

He went to grab my BlackBerry off the treadmill in an attempt to shield me from the horrible discovery.

"What?" I asked, as I took it back from him.

"It was the shellfish," he said, with his arms open for me to run into.

"Nooooooooooooooooooooooooooooooooooo!!!!"

This is the picture I shot with my BlackBerry of him consoling me right there and then on the balcony:

It took several minutes for me to calm down long enough to forward the picture to my team. The hysterical crying was interrupted by hysterical laughing, which I had to cover up with more fake crying, so it became a vicious circle. Luckily, it was a windy day, and Ted is ridiculous.

The rest of the night was more of the same as I was e-mailing with Tom, Jake, and Brad. Brad had to pull over several times on his way to dinner just to gain composure, and Jake kept calling me from his house in the Palisades howling. "This is the stupidest fucking joke in the world.

Ted is going to dump you in the Santa Monica Bay, and I'm going to be laughing so hard I won't be able to do anything about it!"

"I thought you had a soccer game."

"I do, but I'll be laughing at the soccer game."

I told him to stop calling me, because I couldn't keep running out of the room. You could hear him screaming through the phone, and I'd have to jump up and scram every time it rang. "Fuck off," I repeated over and over again.

Ted ran in after the third time Jake called and found me kneeling next to my bed. "Who are you telling to fuck off?"

"My father."

"Oh."

I finally had to take a Lunesta to get to sleep so that I wouldn't have to face him anymore. I woke up the next morning and lay in bed thinking about the difference a day can make. So much had happened in twenty-four hours. So many lives had been touched.

The funeral wasn't until five, so I had to maintain my composure but keep it somewhat real by pretending I was dreading it as well. Ted had been e-mailing everyone at the party to see who was coming to the funeral and he was concerned about who he'd be standing next to during the spreading of the ashes. "I'm worried I'm going to laugh," he kept saying. "Please make sure I'm not anywhere near Tom."

"Don't worry," I wanted to say. "No one else is coming, moron."

But I didn't.

At around four-thirty we headed to the pier. On our way down the ramp, I took a photo of the back of Ted's head and sent it off to everyone who was waiting to hear, with a caption that read "Ted on his way to Dudley's funeral."

I was texting furiously with Johnny Kansas, and he was telling me to stay on Ted's right when we got to the end of the pier. The sign we had made would be set up there on a railing. In order to capture Ted's reaction, we needed to choreograph our arrival perfectly. I realized then that I had forgotten to get flowers and texted Johnny, "We have no flowers."

"Get churros," he replied.

There are churro stands about every two hundred feet at the Santa Monica Pier, so it felt totally natural to yell, "Ted, that's why Dudley liked the pier. The churros. He loved churros!"

"Oh, Jesus Christ. No wonder the dog is fucking dead if he was eating fucking churros."

At this point I was starting to pee a little and kept having to grab my vagina. Luckily it was windy, so it was easy to hide my face behind the hair being blown across it. This was beyond ridiculous, but not as ridiculous as Ted taking a bite out of one of the churros as he crossed back over to where I was.

"What the hell is that?" I asked, pointing at the top of the bitten churro.

"What?" he said, trying to hide the churro under his lapel.

"Those are for Dudley, Ted!"

"But he's dead."

"They wanted to spread the churros with his ashes."

"Chelsea, you can't throw churros over the pier into the water. Dudley would want us to have them. Come on, we're going to be late."

"Just flip that one upside down and don't take another bite."

Fifty yards later we came to the end of the pier, where

there were people scattered about. I immediately saw Johnny facing us, wearing a hoodie and holding a video camera. The sign was to his right. I knew that Ted's keen sense of unawareness would help him take a while to find either one, so I let him run around like a labrador retriever for a few minutes looking for the funeral party while I was trying to stop my urethra from fully discharging all over the Santa Monica Pier. Once he came down from the observation deck, waving his arms in the air, saying, "We missed it! I knew we were going to be late!" I got myself together enough to point to the poster.

"What's that?" I asked.

This was the sign we had made:

Dudley

Two days later I showed the video on *The Tonight Show with Jay Leno*. I haven't played any jokes on Ted since, but Brad did try to persuade me to fake Dudley's death again a week later to see if Ted would believe it. "Say he really died this time!" Brad howled.

Chapter Five

Wedding Chopper

My oldest friend in Los Angeles, Lydia, was getting married, and it was a miracle. I didn't ever expect her to have the wherewithal to actually follow through with a wedding that would require others to attend. She'd been engaged for over two years, and my assumption was that Lydia would approach her nuptials like most other milestones in her life: She would most likely lose interest.

When she finally did notify me about the imminent wedding, it was by an AOL instant message: "Chels, save the date. The wedding is going to be on May 28 in the Palisades!"

"Is this the invitation?" I typed back.

"No! Of course not! What's your address? I'm doing them right now!"

That is how Lydia operated. Her disorderliness had always been her strong suit, and this is coming from someone who hasn't worn a matching pair of socks since Reagan was shot. It wouldn't have been a surprise to me at all if I had received a third-grader's birthday-party invitation to her wedding with the time, date, and location all filled out in block letters on top of preprinted horizontal black lines.

Something along the lines of:

> Occasion: **WEDDING**
> Time: 2–4 P.M.
> Location: **OLIVE GARDEN**

I typed in my address and asked her where the wedding was.

"At Mercedes's."

"The dealership?"

"LOL!!!"

I wasn't joking, but I quickly lost interest in the conversation due to the fact that despite my having spoken to Lydia at great length about misplaced enthusiasm, she insisted on using exclamation points in lieu of periods and continued pairing them with my least favorite invention, LOL. You wouldn't say LOL if you were out to lunch with someone, so why would you write it in an instant message or an e-mail? Just laugh alone in your office or house. I don't need to be notified that you're laughing. If someone is busy laughing, then how do they have the time to be typing the letters LOL? More important, I was midway through a letter to Dear Abby that I'd been construct-ing for the better part of the winter, and I wasn't about to lose my confidence now. I hated that after Abby crossed over, her daughter continued her mother's advice column without changing its name from "Dear Abby" to "Dear Abby's *Fucking* Daughter." It wasn't an easy pill to swallow for those of us who didn't read the column the day Abby's daughter informed readers that she was taking over. The one day she decided to mention her mother was dead hap-pened to coincide with me taking a one-day tie-dying class at the Y, and for months I was left nonplussed by Abby's out-of-left-field advice.

"I'll be there," I wrote back to Lydia. "Wouldn't miss it for the world."

I hadn't spent a lot of time with Lydia since she'd got-ten herself engaged. It wasn't intentional at all; we just sort of drifted apart after she asked me to be a bridesmaid in her wedding, and I coughed loudly enough to pretend I didn't hear her.

I instant-messaged Ivory and asked her what Mer-cedes's was.

"Some new girl Lydia's made friends with who works a pai gow table in Vegas."

"Is she Asian?"

"No, she's blond with Orange County boobs."

"Well, the wedding's at her house, and Lydia should be instant-messaging you with the invitation shortly."

"OMG. I can't wait for Ted to meet Rooster. Do you think they'll duel?"

The thought hadn't occurred to me that I would have to bring Ted to the wedding and that he would meet several people I'd slept with, including Rooster. Rooster is someone I'd accidentally fallen into bed with several times in my twenties. He had taken up with Lydia shortly after I explained to him that I didn't want to deal with a long-distance relationship. The commute from Santa Monica to East Santa Monica was putting too many miles on my car, and his car hadn't started since I met him. Not long after we broke up, we all went to a costume party, and I woke up in an M&M's costume next to him and Lydia moaning.

A plethora of misfits from my waitressing days would surely be in attendance at Lydia's wedding, and it was bound to be fairly horrifying.

Two weeks before the wedding and fourteen days before I purchased her gift, Lydia e-mailed everyone telling us there was a change of venue. She was no longer having the wedding at Mercedes's house. It was now being held at a hotel around the corner from where Ted and I lived.

I e-mailed Ivory. "Lydia just changed the locale of the wedding. No more Merecedes. What do you think her game plan is?"

"With the wedding?"

"With life."

"Just be happy you're not a bridesmaid. You're bringing Ted, right?"

"Yes, I'm bringing Ted. Don't worry. You'll get your day in the sun."

The change of locale was perfect for Ted and me. His major issue other than having to attend a wedding for a person he was convinced he'd never met was that it was on the Saturday night before Memorial Day, and he wanted us to spend the weekend in Laguna Beach.

"How long do we have to stay at the wedding?" Ted asked.

"I don't know. It's probably like four or five hours with the ceremony."

"Four or five hours? We're not going to get down to Laguna until midnight!"

"Well, sorry, Ted, but this isn't a roller-skating party. It's somebody's wedding."

"Who is this person again, and what is in your hair?" he asked, squinting at my head.

"A hair clip, and her name is Lydia. You've met her three times. I've known her since I was twenty, remember?"

"Why does it say Doritos on it?" he inquired upon closer inspection of my head.

"Because it's a chip clip. I couldn't find any hair bands and I wanted to go for a run. Is that okay with you?"

"So what's holding the chips together?" he demanded to know.

"Really, Ted? The chips are more important than me getting some cardio in? I mean, seriously."

"Chelsea, answer the question."

"What is the question?"

"What is holding the chips together?"

"The chips are gone."

"Exactly. Those were the chips for the helicopter, Chelsea. I swear sometimes I feel like I'm living with a refugee."

I didn't want to travel further in the direction this conversation was headed, so I removed the chip clip from my hair and tried to attach it to his penis.

He dodged my attempt, retrieved the clip, and returned it to its proper surroundings.

"We're going to have to get a driver if we're going to be drinking, so if the wedding starts at five, is it okay for the car service to come at seven?"

"I don't know, Ted. Have you ever been to a two-hour wedding?"

"Well, what if I have the car there at seven and then we have the option to leave whenever we want?"

"That will be a waste of money, because we won't be leaving before nine. We need to be there a minimum of four hours. What aren't you copying?"

"But I don't even know any of these people."

"That's not their fault. I know Lydia. She knows me, and unfortunately I know you. You're lucky I'm even allowed to bring a guest. This could have gone either way."

"I don't feel lucky."

Ted has little patience for weddings or birthday parties and has no problem telling the person whose birthday or wedding it is that he doesn't understand why they're celebrating. I, on the other hand, take both of these events very seriously, as long as nothing more than attending and providing gifts is expected of me. I don't like to make speeches, and I don't like to wear assigned clothing. I love birthdays, and I love weddings. Funerals can also be fun, but only with the right mix of refreshments.

Ted and I have always had different policies when it comes to other humans. He's generally not interested in people and doesn't even pretend to try, whereas I am fascinated by anyone and everything, especially if it involves a childhood story about an inappropriate uncle or obesity.

I've attempted to explain to him that just because he doesn't think the anniversary of someone's death holds any real meaning, the person who lost his or her parent most likely feels differently.

"Oh, honey, I'm sorry," he told me on the second anniversary of my mom's death. "I wish I had something to say. I just don't understand what meaning this day holds." Then he rubbed the back of my head while I looked at him the way I looked at my father each time he'd ask me if I was a C or a D cup.

I thought it might be fun for all of us to watch Lydia get married. I've always wanted to see a bride in her wedding dress smoking a cigarette, and I knew Lydia was the one person I could count on to make that dream come true.

A week before the wedding, Ted's assistant happened to find out that there was a helipad on top of the hotel where the wedding was being held. That's when all hell broke loose.

"Chelsea, we could take a helicopter from the hotel in the marina to another hotel in Laguna. We could be in Laguna by seven!"

"The wedding starts at five."

"Eight."

"I'm not bailing early on my friend's wedding because you want to get to a beach community when it's already dark out. What's the point anyway?"

"There's tons of dancing in Laguna, Chelsea! They have discos all along the coast."

I had been dealing with this level of activity for the better part of two years, and his "dancing"—or what I would describe as more of a shuffle-ball rotation—didn't seem to be coming to a simmer at all. Ted loves to dance, and the main problem with this bustle is that he doesn't move his feet, so he ends up looking like a human Tilt-A-Whirl. He maintains this position while also twittering his fingers in the way that someone would do to help someone else back out of a parking space. Then he moves on to what is best described as a basketball dribble, with no basketball and no other players. His eyes are mostly closed, but when they open, they have a look that says, "You're welcome."

I've explained to him that it's an impossible dance to do with a partner and if that is any indication of his skill set, he should maybe reevaluate his choreography. "Who are you waving to?" I've asked him after witnessing this move. "No one is coming over to you."

"People are too intimidated, Chelsea. This is pure Jackson."

Part of me was scared he would perform one of his recitals at the wedding, but another part of me was even more scared that Rooster and Ted would have a dance-off. They're both pretty delusional about their dancing and suffer from the same false confidence that people with Bell's palsy are prone to. The thought of leaving before the Electric Slide suddenly seemed appealing.

"Eight," I told him. "Have the helicopter pick us up at eight."

Helicopters had become our favorite mode of transportation after we saw coverage of that fall's Malibu fires. They're fun, they can land anywhere, and, as a helicopter pilot once told us, "If anything goes wrong on a helicopter, you've got several different ways to save your life." I liked the idea of not dying while flying, and I liked the idea of boarding with a drink in my hand instead of using that hand to take off my belt after getting screamed at by the maniacs at airport security. Plus, the great thing about helicopters is that because you fly so much closer to the ground, you can actually wave to people who think they are in the privacy of their own backyards or Jacuzzis, naked.

The day of the wedding, while Ted was packing, I was in bed watching *The Sisterhood of the Traveling Pants Two*, while I wondered out loud why they didn't call it *The Sisterhood of the Traveling Period*.

"What a gross concept," I said with disdain.

"Why?" Ted asked, looking up at the TV.

"Do they ever wash these pants?" I asked.

"Nope. That's the whole point. They never wash them."

"Don't you think that's foul? These girls are fourteen or fifteen, and one of them was playing soccer in Mexico. I'd rather borrow Linda Hogan's underwear after a day of motorcross."

"The real plot point that they missed is that the jeans fit all the girls perfectly. A lot of people didn't catch that, but I did."

"Ted, it's pretty obvious that they're not all the same size. I'm sure there are other moviegoers that caught that. I caught it, and I'm on the lower end of the IQ seesaw."

"Well, no one's brought it up to me."

"Why would anyone bring it up to *you?*"

"You'd be surprised," Ted reassured me.

"I just don't understand what the point is. I don't like wearing other people's pants, and I certainly don't understand why each of them has such a confused look on her face every time they get a FedEx box. It's obviously the fucking pants."

"All right, sweetie, let's go. We're gonna be late. The wedding's at five, right?"

"Yes." I clicked off the TV and got up. "Where are we going to put our bags?" I asked him. "We can't walk into the hotel with them."

"Why not?"

"Because that's weird. Why are we walking into a hotel that we're not staying at with our bags?"

"We can check them at the front desk and get them when we leave."

"Well, can you at least put your snorkel and swimming equipment in the suitcase? It looks ridiculous coming out of that E! Entertainment beach bag."

"My swimming equipment doesn't fit in any other bag."

The "equipment" he's referring to is a snorkel that comes with a built-in radio, which allows music to enter through his mouthpiece. He also transports two arm paddles, goggles, and a pair of ill-fitting Speedos to whichever hotel we vacation at. He will put all of these items on, then get into a pool and do laps. He expects people who are already settled and relaxing in the pool to move out of his way. If they don't, he'll orbit around the innocent bystanders once in each direction, then get up and argue with them about "pool etiquette," while his snorkel and mask are still in place. It's at this time that I get my belongings together and move to a different area of the resort so that no one thinks we're together.

"Well, we're going to have to take our bags at some point. How would you like to do it?" he asked me.

"I just don't want people to know we're leaving in a helicopter."

"Why not?"

"Because it's a little obnoxious, Ted. I used to wait tables when all these people knew me. I was driving around drunk in a preowned Toyota Echo and getting *Us Weekly* from the public library. It wasn't my finest hour."

"Well, I'm sure they've all grown up, too, right?"

The last time I had seen Rooster and his cohorts was at a bar in Santa Monica where they were head-butting each other to a Fleetwood Mac song and I was supposed to be doing stand-up. After he spotted me, he harangued me for thirty minutes as to why I hadn't written about him in my first book. I explained to him that I didn't think he would want me to but assured him I wouldn't forget him in the next one, which I did not.

Rooster was by far and still is the biggest mess of a group that I hung out with during the latter part of my twenties. He has been given several opportunities to work as a writer's assistant or in some other lower-level position but each time has decided he'd rather wait tables. He's been working on his screenplay for twelve years.

We got to the wedding just before five o'clock and were ushered upstairs to the roof of the hotel for the ceremony. It overlooked the marina, all the boats in the harbor, and the Pacific Ocean beyond.

"This is where the helipad is," Ted exclaimed as he looked around to see where the landing was. "We can fly out of here whenever we want. This is fantastic!"

"Try to stay focused," I told him. "There's Joey. That's Lydia's fiancé."

It was a beautiful day for a wedding, and we made mention of that when we said hello to Joey, even though I wanted to ask him if he knew that his wedding had been canceled and rescheduled via instant message. I looked over at the arranged seats and saw my friend Steph in the back row.

"You're here early," she said as we joined her. "I just watched the best movie. Did you ever see the Muhammad Ali documentary?"

"Of course," Ted interrupted. "Cassius Clay."

"I haven't," I told her. "Is it good? The two things I know nothing about are boxing and the Strongest Man Competition. Or when they throw that rock."

"That's the same competition, sweetie," Ted informed me.

"Have you seen *The Sisterhood of the Traveling Pants*?" I asked Steph.

"One or two?"

"That was a sequel to another movie?" I asked in disbelief.

"Yes, Chelsea. In the movie business, the 'two' implies a sequel," Ted revealed.

I turned to face him. "Can you please shut the fuck up? Obviously I know that. This is a different set of circumstances, considering the subject matter of the movie. The two at the end of the title *could* have been tipping a hat to the act of going number two. Ever think of *that*, smarty pants? Anyway," I said, shifting my attention back to Steph, "what were you saying?"

"The documentary's amazing," Steph said. "You should hear Ali speak. It's pretty intense. He's like a prophet."

"Is he the one with the grill?"

"No. That's George Foreman," Ted explained, patting his hair. "It's a pretty fantastic item. He also just came out with a panini press. You want to talk sandwiches, I'll give you a sandwich. George is a great guy. Known him for years." Then he looked at the helipad's windsock. "If this wind hits thirty knots, I'm gonna need access to a hair-brush. I may have to go down and get our bags."

People were starting to file in, and it looked as if the event was getting started. I tried to avoid eye contact with all the usual suspects, since I knew I would have plenty of opportunities in the next couple of hours to reminisce about the days when Ecstasy and Vicodin took up most of my mornings and early afternoons.

Instead I opted to interrogate Steph about the documentary and find out as much as I could about why anyone would have the desire to get hit in the face for a living.

"The Tyson documentary is pretty amazing, too," she added. "Have you seen that?"

"No, but I would be more interested in seeing one on Muhammad Ali," I told her.

"The Tyson documentary is very telling, Chelsea," Ted argued. "You see a side of him you didn't expect to see."

"Did you see it?" Steph asked Ted.

"Of course he didn't see it," I told her.

"You don't know if I saw it, Chelsea." Then he turned to Steph. "I have not seen it, but that's what everyone's saying."

"It's true," she agreed. "You do see a different side that I didn't know he had."

"Well," I informed then both, "I'll tell you what I do know. I know that Mike Tyson has a tattoo on his eye, and that's a pretty good indicator that all cylinders are not firing."

Ted had lost interest in the conversation and had moved on to his BlackBerry. "Do you think I have time to run to the market for some chips and salsa to have on the chopper?" he whispered.

"No. The wedding is about to start and we're on the roof of a hotel. And please don't refer to it as a chopper. You're not Al Roker, and I'm not a Doppler radar."

I looked back to see all the groomsmen lined up at the perimeter of the roof, ready for their walk. When the music started, Ted was still on his BlackBerry, so I elbowed him in the ribs.

"I'm just ordering the chips and salsa."

Lydia was bawling before she even hit the aisle and her soon-to-be-husband looked like he was going to vomit. Ted made a half-assed attempt to cover his mouth and leaned in.

"Is he okay?"

"Shut up."

"That's the groom, right?" he asked, pointing to the only man in a tuxedo standing next to the justice of the peace, whose hand he had shaken five minutes earlier. "He looks sick."

The justice of the peace was clearly on sabbatical from his duties as a Carnival Cruise director. The enthusiasm with which he was conducting himself was about as believable as a three-legged alligator that also does magic. He obviously had no history with Lydia and her fiancé but was acting like he had rescued them both from orphanages and raised them for thirty years. He looked like John Ritter if John Ritter had been an asshole. I had to assume that his name was Tito, and not the black kind. He was white and the type of person who announces "I love meat" every time he's in an Outback Steakhouse.

I imagined that Lydia had likely hired this guy after a friend of hers had promised to get an online marriage license and then forgot to.

After Tito said that Lydia's love for Joey was something that could only be found in a Shakespearean play, I watched as Joey's face twitched. It was pretty windy, so some of the stuff I couldn't hear, but luckily the wind died down for this: "Joey, the passion you feel for Lydia is something only you and Lydia can know about, and you are agreeing today to never allow your passion to flee from the sanctity of this day, or from Lydia...." I looked at Ted. His head was cranked so far away from me, as he was trying not to laugh, that my only recourse was to bite down on one of my knuckles. Then came two knuckles, and then, before long, my entire fist was in my mouth. "Love is like a Ferris wheel. Round and round it goes, and sometimes it will get stuck right at the top, and sometimes it will skip past the spot at the bottom where ticketholders are supposed to get on and off. No pun intended."

"Oh, my God," Ted groaned.

I removed my fist, wiped the slobber onto my dress, and whispered to Ted, "And sometimes, if you're Chuy, you can't even get on the Ferris wheel."

"...Remember, the world is a place where two lovers..." and then a thundering noise came from the sky. *Thwap, thwap, thwap, thwap, thwap, thwap, thwap, thwap, thwap.* It was growing louder and louder, and it sounded like someone had gotten a flat tire. I looked up and saw a helicopter.

"Oh, my God."

"No," said Ted.

"This better not be our ride," I said through gritted teeth.

He lowered his sunglasses on his nose in order to be clear about what he saw. "That can't be ours, it's too early." The helicopter was getting closer and didn't look like it was turning around. I closed my eyes and imagined a world with only dolphins and Abigail Breslin.

"Ted."

"What? No, that's someone else's."

"No one else ordered a helicopter. I can guarantee that."

"You don't know that, Chelsea."

"Yes I do. You are the only person who would do that. You and the coast guard."

The helicopter was headed straight for us, but I believed in my state of panic and horror that if I stared the helicopter straight in the eye the way people suggest you do when coming into contact with a bear, it would eventually lose interest and head in the other direction.

"Oh, my God, is that going to land here?" Steph asked

as softly as was permissible in the current hailstorm of conditions.

I had one of Ted's balls in my grip. "You are the *worst.*"

"No, no, no, no," he repeated as he released my hold on his testicle while keeping both eyes on the incoming aircraft. He was now squeezing my hand and saying, "I'm so sorry. I really don't think anyone can even hear it with the wind."

I didn't look around to see if this was true for fear of finding out that it wasn't. Taking the wind into consideration, it was plausible that depending on where you were seated, you might be oblivious to the fact that a helicopter was about to land on our heads. I looked down at my toes to try to come up with some believable explanation as to why a helicopter pilot was about to get out of a helicopter on the roof of a hotel, in the middle of my friend's wedding, and most likely say our names.

"They can't land. It's a total safety hazard. They're not going to land in the middle of a wedding," Ted assured me. The *thwap-thwap-thwap* was getting closer, and more heads were turning. It was definitely only the seats on our side that could hear it; the other side seemed lost in Tito's *Snow White and the Seven Dwarfs* comparison. Finally Ted threw his hands violently up in the air with a wave that would only be necessary if he was directing a Hannah Montana video. Nonetheless, it turned out to be an effective movement, because within thirty seconds the helicopter made a hard right and was veering away from the building, back toward the marina.

"Oh, thank God," I said, with my hands in prayer position. Then I attempted to do the sign of the cross, but me being a half Jew, my hands crossed signals and I ended up slapping Ted's earlobe. Right then I saw Ivory for the first time that afternoon; she had the very familiar look on her face that implied she had no intention of making eye contact with me. I hadn't told her about the helicopter, but it was clear she was one of the people who'd heard it. We had vowed a long time ago to never again sit next to each other at weddings, funerals, or quinceañeras, because of my inability to be serious at important events. I tried to get her attention, but she insisted on respecting the fact that we were at a wedding and locking eyes with the gazebo under which Lydia and Joey were getting married. This wasn't the first time Ivory had disappointed me, and it surely wouldn't be the last.

I moved closer to Ted. "The only thing that will make this day any better is if that minister guy turns around after he's done marrying them and jumps off the roof of this hotel."

"I mean, really. He is astonishing."

"His name is Tito, and he's Caucasian."

Once Tito pronounced them man and wife, I knew we were in the clear, except for the face rape Lydia applied to Joey's face.

Kisses swapping DNA should be saved for the bedroom, living room, or media lounge. "Ew," Ted and I both said in unison.

We finally got up and headed toward Ivory. "How's your hair?" she asked Ted.

"Not great. Not optimal conditions."

Ivory explained to us that there had been some confusion about which room the reception was being held in and that the room they had promised her was not the room she was getting.

"What kind of operation is this?" I asked.

"Let's go get cocktails!" Ted exploded, with his fists pumped.

Ivory loves Ted and Ted loves Ivory, and there were plenty of times I thought they should just go off and marry each other. The three of us said our casual hellos to everyone as we passed them on foot doing about thirty miles an hour toward the elevators. I had heard Rooster out of the corner of one of my ears and mentioned to Ivory that we might as well get the introduction between him and Ted over with, but she thought it would be more of a shitstorm if everyone was properly liquored up.

"You're right," I said, and grabbed her shoulder. "You're an amazing friend."

We grabbed the closest table to the bar that was available and were joined by Lionel and Sharona, a couple Ivory and I both knew, but who were much closer with Lydia.

Two hot messes who had one baby and one on the way. It took a few minutes for Sharona to lower herself down into the chair, with Lionel and Ted assisting.

"Is there table service, or do we have to go up to the bar?" Lionel asked, before Sharona had completely lodged her ass into the seat. Then he looked over, smiled at her, and punched her in the shoulder. "Look at ya, ya fat monster!"

The five us were now apparently sitting together. After Sharona told us her due date was the next day and we deduced that there was no table service, Ted volunteered to go up to the bar and get everyone a drink. When Sharona ordered a vodka with cranberry while resting both hands on her belly, Ted nodded, looked at her belly, then looked back at me.

"I'll take the same," I told him.

Ted came back saying he had a found a waiter who would be by momentarily to take our drink orders. After Lionel and Ivory both made mention of a helicopter almost flying over the wedding, Ted and I looked up at the sky in confusion and said we hadn't even noticed.

Lionel was telling us a story about how he and Sharona had gotten into a pretty serious accident on a drive to Santa Barbara the weekend before. "The guy in front of us slammed on his brakes in the middle of the freeway, and we were able to stop, but when I looked in my rearview mirror, the woman behind us was texting and didn't see that we had stopped in time for her to stop. She tried at the last minute, but it was too late, and she slid right underneath our car, and the car was airborne for what felt like a minute. Nothing scarier than looking at your child in the rearview mirror screaming and not being able to protect him." At this exact moment, Ted spotted a waiter walking by and ordered a cocktail.

"I'll take a Belvedere rocks, splash of cran, splash of orange. Great. Thanks."

When he looked back at us and saw that all our mouths were open, he seemed surprised. "Oh, I'm sorry, did anyone else want anything?"

I waited until we were alone with Ivory walking to the reception before I confronted him. "Listen up, shitstain. Under no circumstances are you allowed to order a cocktail in the middle of someone telling a story about a car accident that *he and his child* were involved in."

"I didn't want to risk having the waiter go away!"

"I understand how important drinks are, but if someone is telling a story about a car being airborne with him and his child in it, the sensitive thing to do is at least pretend you care and avoid interrupting the story with a cocktail order."

"How about an appetizer?"

Ivory was no help, because she found this exchange hilarious and thinks Ted is the funniest person in the world. I disagree with that assessment and am strongly opposed to anyone suggesting it.

We were greeted at the reception by three industrial-strength box fans outside each of the three entrances to the mini-ballroom. When I asked one of the waiters what the fans were for, he said that the air-conditioning in that room had broken.

Ivory sat down next to me sweating and grinding her teeth. "Guess who's here?"

"Lance Bass."

"Better. Calypso."

Calypso was the drug dealer that this whole group of people relied on. When I asked Ivory if he'd been called for delivery purposes or if he was invited to the wedding as a guest, she didn't have an answer. "Maybe he came to fix the air-conditioning," she suggested.

I looked over and saw him leaving Rooster's table. Rooster was also grinding his teeth, which meant one of two things. I knew that Ted wouldn't want anything, but I was definitely interested in getting my hands on some sort of muscle relaxer or painkiller.

Ivory went to tell Calypso I would like his next stop to be my table. Steph came and sat down next to me and asked if everyone at the wedding was on drugs. I told her I doubted that Joey and Lydia were on anything other than an emotionally passionate high, and I also didn't think either set of parents would be high, since they're all in their sixties and none of them is Keith Richards.

As soon as Calypso made his way over, Steph got up and let him take her seat. Calypso was wearing his version of a suit: light blue and a cotton/poly blend, with a black shirt and high-top sneakers. He was Mexican.

"Hey there, what kind of goodies you got?" I asked him.

Calypso half opened his jacket to reveal a pharmacy-like arrangement of all the different products he was peddling. "I got blow, 'shrooms, MDMA, Ecstasy, weed, Ambien—what do ya need?"

Ted tapped me on the shoulder. "Can I talk to you for a second, Chelsea?"

We got up, walked outside the reception room, and stood behind one of the fans. "What is your game plan with that guy?"

"I don't know yet. I'm trying to see if he has any Vicodin."

"I assume Calypso is a pharmacist?" Ted inquired.

"Yes, he's with Cobra. My calf hurts."

"Well, whatever you think you need, please get double, because I do not ever want to see 'Calypso' again." Ted is adamant about denouncing drugs, but I believe in my heart of hearts that if he worked as a bricklayer instead of as a CEO, our lives would be more prone to illegal activities and our relationship would benefit exponentially from the cocktail of chemicals.

I went back to the table and asked Calypso if he had any Vicodin, which he did. I bought two and split one with myself at the table.

Three hours later my dream of seeing a bride smoking a cigarette and Ivory's dream of seeing Rooster introduce himself to Ted in the middle of the dance floor both came true. Ted came up to me drenched in his own dance sweat.

"That Poultry guy will not leave me alone. Can we go now? Seriously, Chelsea, you're lucky I came into your life when I did. You'd probably be living under a freeway somewhere."

We headed to the lobby to grab our bags. Ivory and Rooster ran up to us at the front desk, while I pretended to be looking at room rates.

Rooster leaned in and grabbed Ted's shoulder. "Where do you guys think you're going? Fred, I was just going to ask you to dance. I like that little 'Thriller' move you do."

"We're going to Laguna for the weekend," Ted told him.

"By car," I added.

Not one to take a hint, Ted immediately jumped in and asked me, "What do you mean?"

"We were just walking outside to get a taxi to take us to Laguna, *Fred*," I said loudly.

So instead of going up to the roof where we were expected, we were escorted outside by Ivory and Rooster, got into a taxi, rode around the block, came back to the hotel, and then ran to the elevators as fast as we could.

Once we were airborne, Ted told me that he thought Poultry still had feelings for me. "You should see if he wants to get back together, and then you'll never have to ride in a helicopter again. You can ride around in his go-cart."

"His name is Rooster."

"He actually seemed like he'd be a nice guy if he wasn't so hammered. I could barely understand a word he said. He kept moving his mouth around in circles."

"Yeah, he must have been tired."

"And by the way, Ms. Handler, he and I turned out to have more in common than you would think."

"Oh, really?"

"Yes, really. For your information it turns out I'm not the only one who missed a day of work when Michael Jackson died."

"I'm sorry?"

"He didn't work the next day either, because he was too upset."

"No, Ted. He didn't work the next day either because he doesn't have a job."

Ted opened up the bag of chips he had managed to have on board.

"Now, let's focus on us. We have a choice for dancing tonight. We can either go to a dance club I found online or just dance in our room if you want. I brought my iPod dock and just downloaded all of Earth, Wind & Fire's greatest hits."

"Let's stay in tonight," I said, envisioning all the twenty- and thirty-something stares I would have to endure while Ted slid across the dance floor, crying if a Michael Jackson song came on. "Although you *are* already warmed up. Maybe we should go out."

"Nah, let's save it," he said in complete seriousness. "We don't want to spoil people."

I looked down at the coastline and at the waves crashing on the shore and said something I never thought I'd say. "I miss Tito."

Chapter Six

Water Olympics

Like any self-respecting brother-and-sister combo, Greg and I decided to eat some mushrooms. We were out to dinner in Martha's Vineyard with my sister the Mormon and her fiancé, Mike.

When the server came over, Mike ordered a Heineken, I ordered my standard vodka with lemon, and Greg decided to go with a double-gay Bay Breeze.

"When do you think you'll be starting your first period?" I asked my brother.

"Chelsea, I think we both know I've been getting my period since the third grade."

Greg is not a gay man, but he has some very gay qualities, which he is not only quick to admit to but even quicker to embrace. Today he is married to a Russian woman and has three small Russian sons who live in New Jersey and speak with thick Russian accents. This dinner took place long before we lost him to Communism and room-temperature orange juice.

"Can you two please not talk about periods?" Sloane piped up, looking sideways at Mike.

I didn't know Mike very well at the time, but what I did know was that trying to get a conversation started with him was like trying to go sleigh-riding in a straitjacket. He was extremely quiet.

Greg and I are not quiet and have never pretended to be. We both have extremely unfortunate personalities and thrive on embarrassing anyone we're in a room with. Somehow we have both managed to carve out lives for ourselves and yet maintain an attitude of utter disrepair. He is a certified public accountant, and I have a real life.

"When do you think you'll get our sister knocked up?" Greg asked Mike, taking a bite out of the cherry that came in his drink. Sloane was five years older than Mike and was interested in getting married, penetrated, and knocked up. In that order. The best news about Mike was that, unlike Sloane, he had not been captured by Mormons.

From what I could gather by his facial expression, Mike didn't seem to have any problem with the topics of penetration or menstruation.

"I have mushrooms," I announced.

"Oh, that's nice," Sloane said.

"Where did you get them?" Greg inquired.

"From a drug dealer."

He put his hand out. "Please give me some."

I pulled a Ziploc bag from of my purse. "Would you like some mushrooms, Mike?"

Mike looked at Sloane, who looked back at him like he was four years old.

"Nah," he said, "that's okay."

Greg pointed his finger in Mike's face, sternly. "Mike, if you want some mushrooms, my suggestion is that you have some mushrooms. These are your last months as a free man."

"Mike is not doing mushrooms," announced Sloane.

"Fine," I said, making two small piles on the table. I then proceeded to eat my portion of the mushrooms as I perused the menu, trying to decide how much food would prevent me from getting a good high.

"That's really nice, you guys. You're just gonna get high at the table and then what?"

"We'll probably end up robbing a liquor store, Sloane. Mushrooms can be very violent," Greg told her with no inflection, grimacing at the flavor of the drugs. "These taste like a moose's asshole."

"Uh, I wouldn't bring up anyone's asshole at the same time you're holding a Bay Breeze with your pinky pointed toward the sun. It's better to mix it with some food. Wanna split the seafood tower?"

Greg nodded in agreement and then leaned in. "Do you

know that in five states it is legal to mail your dump to another person, but if you do it more than once, you can get arrested?"

Sloane lifted her elbow to the table, resting her chin on her fist, and looked in any direction but ours. "This is just great. This is lovely dinner conversation, by the way. I'm so glad we did this."

I for one couldn't have been more fascinated. "You can mail a shadoobie to another person?"

"That's correct."

Even Mike was flabbergasted. "Wow. That's pretty intense."

"But, Chelsea," Greg said sternly, "you cannot do it twice."

"Well, that's stupid," I told him. "Who would need to do it twice? If the person you sent it to the first time doesn't understand that a shadoobie in the mail means that *that friendship is on the rocks*, he certainly isn't going to figure it out the second time. That would be a total waste of a stamp."

"Or two stamps, Chelsea. Depending on just how big that shadoobie is."

"So where are you guys going to go when you start hallucinating?" Sloane asked. "Back to the house to hang out with Mom and Dad?"

"Don't tell Mom and Dad that we did mushrooms, Sloane."

That was the last thing I remember saying before I

started seeing flying Chinese babies. Sloane claims that Greg and I got up from the table before our food came and started dancing in the middle of the restaurant, together.

After she and Mike finished their meal, she came over to us and told us they were leaving and that we could take a cab home. Then she said that she told me, "There is no music playing, and you and Greg are related." I do in fact remember dancing, but I have a hard time believing there was no music.

About four hours later, I found myself in a cab back to my parents' house without Greg. I was still pretty high, but now the Chinese babies were at my eye level and were on foot.

At some point in the evening, my brother and I had separated. After the restaurant we'd gone to a bar across the street where they actually had an area designated for dancing, called a dance floor. I'm pretty confident I spent most of the night humiliating myself on it, but I had no idea when or where Greg had removed himself.

During the ten-minute cab ride to our house, I became increasingly concerned over Greg's whereabouts. Although I have been lucky enough not to ever have had a bad reaction to the drugs I've experimented with, some people are not as fortunate. It dawned on me that he could have been freaking out somewhere in a roadside bush. Once we pulled onto the dirt road that led to our house, the cabdriver recognized the road and said he had just dropped another person here an hour earlier. Thank God, I thought, and was able to go back to my previous jubilation of being in a paranoia-free zone of euphoria. This wasn't the first time Greg and I had crossed paths with the same driver in the hours of darkness.

A year earlier we had some hillbilly cousins from a small town outside Portland, Oregon, decide that it would be a good idea to get married. Neither of us had been invited to the wedding, but Greg called me in California and asked me if I wanted to crash. I had no desire to be in attendance at an affair that was most likely going to take place at either a VFW hall or a Chili's. He persisted in convincing me that we should go together and that it would be good material. Material for what was never specified.

I had no real commitments at the time, being twenty and just recently moved to Los Angeles, where I was in between thinking I should get a job and getting one.

"Fine," I finally said. "You need to use your miles for my ticket, and I'm not staying at a Super 8 or at one of our 'pseudo' cousins' trailers." I had to be very specific with Greg, as he is prone to spending as little money as possible, and that is something, try as I might, I cannot get behind.

"I want nice dinners, Greg. No Colonel Sanders shit." I had nothing against the colonel himself but am very leery of the idea that there was ever a colonel in the first place. What kind of colonel would allow his establishment to turn into such a mockery? After a lengthy negotiation, we compromised on moderately priced dining, as long as I agreed to at least one serving of the colonel's chicken, or, as I had grown to refer to it, Kentucky Fried Pony.

The wedding "reception" took place at a karaoke bar, which is one thing I do not and will not participate in. I've found that many of the people who have a passion for karaoke too often have misplaced confidence, which can become aggressive and at times border on sadistic. I know my limits, and karaoke is where I draw the line. I wouldn't put anyone through the hell of listening to me sing a song, and I sure as shit wouldn't wait in line to do it.

The bartender told me the kitchen was closed, so I looked around for my brother, who was hard to find in the sea of mullets that were related to me. Since this wedding celebration hadn't provided any food, it was my duty to provide myself with some sustenance.

I looked in the closed kitchen. The perfect condition I like a kitchen to be in when I decide to test out my culinary skills. I opened the freezer, got out some hamburger patties and some frozen onion rings, and then looked around for something to cook these items in or on. Soon after, I gave up and walked outside. I was standing in front of the bar, looking at the adjacent strip malls and intersections, with my forefinger pointed at my temple, trying to find something that piqued my palate.

Taco Bell was in the near distance, but I was in no mood to walk more than one-eighth of a mile, so I waved down the first car I saw.

A man in a dark brown Toyota low-rider sort of sedan

stopped. When I leaned in, I saw that he had a nice smile, weighed close to four hundred pounds, and was solely responsible for the car being low-riding. "Any chance I could get a ride to that Taco Bell right over there?"

"Sure thing, kiddo, hop right in.

"*You* are a lifesaver." I smiled, calculating how many tacos I could buy with five dollars. I walked around to the passenger-side door and hopped in. "I know it's not far, but I'm at this wedding with no food, and I'm starving." I looked at his body out of the corner of my eye and concluded that if circumstances called for it, he would be able to crush me. However, he would have to catch me first, and unless he was some sort of Transformer or fat vampire, this was unlikely in his condition.

He was a very nice man indeed, and I liked the way his big fat body leaned when we were turning in to the intersection. He asked me where I was from, and when I told him New Jersey, he slapped his thigh. I couldn't tell which because together they equaled one gargantuan slab of meat. I wondered how many chicken tacos the geniuses at Taco Bell could make out of his carcass. Realizing this would require a measuring instrument, which I didn't pack, I pressed on to the task at hand.

"Well, what kind of coincidence is that?" he was saying. "I just drove a fella from New Jersey to the very same Taco Bell. He was an accountant. Real nice guy, real hungry."

"Was his name Greg?"

"Yes, it was," and then he slapped his leg again. "He

done try and walk through the drive-through, and when they sent him away, he came and hailed me down in the middle of the road!"

"That sounds about right." We were at the window now, so my first goal was to get in my order for two Taco Supremes. Then I asked my date if he wanted anything.

"Oh, God no. I can't eat this crap."

"I'll take three, then!" I yelled back into the window.

When we pulled back in to the parking lot of the karaoke bar, I spotted Greg sitting on the top part of a bench facedown in a burrito.

We pulled up right in front of him, and with half of a taco in my mouth I yelled, "Greg, look who I found!"

Greg looked up and walked over to the car with a big smile on his face. He liked this kind of nonsense very much. "Good evening, Chelsea, I see you've met my friend Large Luke."

Greg still keeps in touch with Luke to this day, because that's how Greg is. He finds extreme joy in people who no one else would pay attention to. Then he'll invite them to stay at his house for the weekend while his wife hides in the bedroom with their three children and makes porridge.

By the time I got back to my parents' house, it was midnight. I walked in the door to find Sloane and Mike sitting at the kitchen table each having a bowl of cereal and my other brother Ray watching a Mets game in the living room.

"Is Greg here?" I inquired.

"No," Ray said, looking up from the game, eyeing the matted hair stuck to my forehead. "Where are you just coming from, a pole vaulting class?" I had gotten quite a workout dancing and had probably lost a significant amount of water. I was laser-focused on weighing myself.

"Don't ask, Ray," Sloane interrupted. "I thought Greg was with you."

"He was, but we lost each other, and the cabdriver said he dropped him off here an hour ago."

"I haven't seen him," she said, and then asked Ray if he had.

Ray has the demeanor of someone who really isn't bothered by much and would greatly prefer to watch the Mets lose one game after another while he idly sits by. "Heartbreakers," he mumbles every time a game ends. "These guys are killing me."

"Well, I'm a little concerned, Sloane," I said. "I don't know where he is."

"He's thirty-four," Ray said. "I'm sure he's fine. Chelsea, why don't you go into the kitchen and have some Gatorade? You look a little pale and stupid."

"I'm going to check in the basement," I announced, and headed toward the sliding glass door that leads to our front deck. "Ray, come with me. I'm scared."

"Wait for this inning to end."

"Sloane, come with me. I'm scared."

Sloane got up and came outside. We walked around the deck to the set of stairs that leads down to the basement, and we saw all of Greg's clothes folded neatly on one of the steps, with his sneakers next to them.

"Oh, my God!" I screamed, grabbing Sloane. "He probably swam to Chappy!" Our dilapidated house in Martha's Vineyard is positioned in front of Katama Bay. On the other side of it lies Chappaquiddick. Chappy, for short. This is the smaller island that became famous for the incident where a drunk Ted Kennedy drove his car off a small bridge and left a woman there to drown. Silly Kennedys.

The distance between our beach and Chappy's beach is a little under a mile. Greg likes to swim through all the boats docked in the bay to the other side. This activity performed sober and in the daytime is risky for anyone other than a salmon.

"Oh, my gosh," Sloane said.

"We have to go get him. He'll drown." I sprang into full panic mode, and it was infectious. Sloane was instantly on board with my paranoia, and we ran inside to get the boys.

"You guys, Greg went down to the water and swam to Chappy in the dark. We have to go get him!"

This was Mike's first visit to our summerhouse, and he had no idea if swimming to Chappy was good or bad, but he definitely reacted with the appropriate look of panic in his eyes. He was already perplexed by the fact that my parents had a house on Martha's Vineyard, even though my father hadn't had a real job in a decade and dressed like a circus carny.

Mike glanced at Ray, who was still reclined on the sofa. "He's fine. He does it all the time."

"Not at night, Ray!" I wailed.

"He's on mushrooms!" Sloane added.

"Who has mushrooms?" Ray asked.

"I did," I told him. "Greg and I split them. There aren't any more."

He looked back at the TV. "Well, no wonder you're acting schizophrenic, Chels. Why don't you go weigh yourself or something?"

"I am not being schizo," I told him. "We need to go down to the water and see if he's okay. That is our brother, Ray!"

"Mom hid the scale," Sloane announced.

"What do you mean?" I asked her. "You can't hide a scale."

"She hid it because she thinks you weigh yourself too much. You're becoming obsessed."

"Where did she put the scale, Sloane?"

"I have no idea. She just said she was hiding it."

"Check in the washing machine," Ray suggested. My mother pulled this number often with the TV remote control when she was sick of watching my father sitting on his ass all day. More often than not, she forgot about it and ended up washing several remote controls throughout the summer.

The scale turned out to be in the dryer, so I took it out and slid it underneath for later, where I knew no one would ever see it. Then I refocused myself on the task at hand.

"Okay, Sloane," I said, clapping my hands. "Ray, are you coming or not?"

"Girls, it's a bay. There are no sharks or manatees or whatever you think is going to get him. He's done it a million times. Please relax. If he gets tired, he can just hop on one of the boats. Seriously, girls. You are giving me severe headacheage."

My next move was to burst into tears, which caused Sloane to also start crying. Mike walked over and, with absolutely no conviction, put his hand out to comfort us but then retracted it and, not knowing what else to do, crossed his arms.

"Let's go," Sloane said, and we headed back out the sliding door. "Mike, go down to the basement and get a flashlight."

The water was about a hundred yards from our deck. Mike met us at the front of the house with an industrial-size flashlight. From there we headed across the lawn to the dirt road and found the path that went down to the water.

Sloane and I were still crying as we ran like lunatics through the pitch black with the flashlight bouncing all over the place. The tree-canopied path that leads to the water is riddled with thornbushes, poison ivy, and wet marsh grass that may as well be a giant placenta.

Sloane was holding on to my ponytail, which was becoming looser and looser as a result. The first time I veered to avoid a branch I saw at the last minute, she was able to avoid it, too, but my ponytail completely came loose, and her second and third interactions with branches weren't as fortuitous.

"Shit!" I screamed, trying to assist Mike in helping her get to her feet after her first tumble. Everyone in our family suffers from extreme lack of coordination and an immoderate amount of clumsiness. Even though this is a path Sloane and I had been down hundreds of times during broad daylight, the familiarity of it was completely lost on us. Add to the mix a wooded marshy path in the middle of the black night and you might as well have put us in a minefield with Bose headphones and a water gun.

At the end of the path was a small wooden dock that took you over the marshiest part and fell out on the beach. Once on the beach, I started yelling Greg's name.

"Greg! Greeeggg! Greg!"

Sloane chimed in with screams of her own, and so did Mike, who was surprisingly becoming the forefront of Operation Seafood Tower Rescue.

"We have to get out there. We need a boat," I told them.

"We can take one of the dinghies," she said, shining the flashlight on a bunch of little rowboats that people used to get from the beach to their bigger boats.

Mike grabbed the closest one, flipped it over, and pushed it into the water. It had two benches in the middle and a smaller bench on each end, and two sets of oars inside. The perfect mode of transportation if you were a family of midgets on *The Amazing Race* trying to make it through Willy Wonka's Chocolate River.

I took control of the flashlight so Mike could grab the first set of oars and start rowing while Sloane took the other. After ten solid minutes of huffing and puffing and becoming completely dizzy, it occurred to us that we had made no progress at all and were in the same exact place we started.

"Sloane!" Mike yelled. "You're supposed to be rowing forward like me, not canceling out my row!"

"I can't see which way you're rowing!" They were seated with their backs to each other, and I was in the middle as the captain.

I grabbed the oars out of her hands and started rowing myself.

It was impossible to see anything beyond the three to four feet the flashlight illuminated, and impossible to tell if we were making any headway.

"Chelsea, find a boat or landmark with the flashlight so we have a point of reference," Mike ordered.

"Done. There's a red anchor buoy thingy right there."

"They're all red, Chelsea. That doesn't help us!" Sloane screamed.

"Then *you* find something, you big Mormon."

Mike ordered us to just keep rowing in the same direction so that we would eventually make some progress in getting over to the other side. He also told us both to stop arguing and to focus on saving our brother from a dark, untimely death.

Sloane decided it would be a good idea to come back to where I was seated at the end of the boat and supervise.

"Get out of the back of the boat, you dumbass. It's gonna fill with water!" Before this sentence even left my mouth, Mike had fallen out of the boat, because half of it was already submerged in water. Sloane fell out next. I grabbed the front end of the rowboat while it got higher and higher but let go right before it capsized. Now we were all in the water with our flip-flops floating beside us. I took this opportunity to relieve myself.

Mike had started swimming toward the dinghy and was trying to turn it back over.

I looked at Sloane, who was treading water in a manner that suggested she wasn't going to be afloat for much longer. "You really are a dick," I told her as I swam over to her. She grabbed my shoulders, pushing my whole head underwater.

"Sorry!" she yelped as I went down.

I released her from my grip and swam back up to the surface. "What is wrong with you?"

"I'm so tired. I think I have whiplash."

"Well, I'm not a fucking flotation device. You can't just push on me and expect me to keep coming back up. You are so weak. Lie on your back, and I'll hold you. That's easier." We did just that, and I looked over to see where Mike was. I noticed that the water went from cool to luke-warm a little too quickly. "Are you peeing?"

"Yes," Sloane answered. "But just for a second."

"There's an oar!" I yelled to Mike.

"I'm right here, just a minute." Mike was now visible,

and I could see him dragging the dinghy back in our direction. Once over by us, he flipped the boat into its upright position. "Where are the oars?"

"Fuck. I just saw one." I swam and grabbed what looked like an oar from farther away but turned out to be the flashlight. The dead, clearly non-waterproof flashlight.

"Chelsea, can you please stop swearing?" Sloane said as her head sank under water.

"Fuck off, Sloane. We need to find the oars. Greeeee-gggggggg!!!!"

Greg's first response came in the form of high-pitched squealing and what sounded like brooding laughter. It all felt eerily reminiscent of the movie *Deliverance*, but in a much nicer part of the country and with yachts.

"Oh, my God! Is that him? Where are you? Are you okay?"

It *was* Greg, and he was laughing in a singsong kind of way. "Hello, girls" . . . and then more creepy laughing.

"Where are you?!" Sloane and I screamed in unison. There were echoes across the bay, so it was hard to decipher where his voice was coming from. The flashlight was useless, and our only sense of direction at this point came from Greg's maniacal laughing.

Between Mike and me, we somehow managed to get Sloane back into the boat, face-first. "My nose!" she yelled as she landed. Had I been less high, I would have remembered the time she capsized a kayak with only herself in it. "You are by far the most useless person in this family."

"You know what, Chelsea?" Mike chimed in. "We're all in this together. We need to focus on rescuing Greg. She's doing her best."

I liked that Mike was defending my sister. She clearly wasn't able to defend herself. Mike was a good egg, and I liked a guy who didn't speak often but meant it when he did. And further, like Rihanna, I respect a guy who yells at me.

"You're right, Mike." Then I smacked Sloane on the back of the head when he turned around.

"Girls! Look out, look out wherever you are . . . ," Greg sang.

"We're almost there," Mike yelled back. He was now using one arm to row while I was rowing with an oar.

We got close enough to hear Greg splashing in the water but were still unable to see him. "I'm right over here, dumbasses, on the dock." Greg was clearly enjoying this, and it dawned on me that I hadn't eaten in hours. I checked to see if my hip bone was protruding. Finally some good news. My thoughts drifted back to Large Luke, and I wondered if he had ever lived as a sea animal and felt his hip bone protrude. It seemed unlikely.

"I think I see him," Sloane announced. "It's him."

I craned my neck to try to see what she saw, then jumped into the water to swim over to him. "I'm in the water, give me your hand."

Greg reached out to grab me out of the water and helped me up onto the dock. "Welcome, kids, how was your trip? Mike, how blown away are you by Sloane's maritime skills? She's a regular naval officer, don't you think?" Greg was his usual sarcastic, obnoxious self, and it was clear to all of us that this whole escapade had been a waste of everyone's time.

I got up from where I was sitting on the edge of the dock, intending to slap Greg across the back of the head. That's when I saw that he was completely naked. That's also when I jumped back into the water. "You are so gross, Greg. He's naked, Sloane. Close your eyes."

"Ew!"

Mike had finally had enough of this voyage and was clearly exhausted from his captaining, and I heard him utter his first curse word: "This is a fucking joke."

I grabbed Sloane, and we swam the short bit to the beach and stormed off into the dunes back to the house.

"Girls, we're on Chappy!" Greg called, chasing after us. "Where do you think you're going? We have to go back to the other side."

I had become so disoriented and tired that I didn't even know we had actually accomplished getting to the other side of the bay. Sloane slumped down in the sand and started to whimper. I looked down at her and told her to have some dignity. I took any anger I had left out on the culprit himself.

"You're an asshole for swimming in the middle of the night. We thought something had happened to you. We shoplifted a fucking boat, you dickfucker."

"Maybe you're the asshole, Chelsea, for swimming across a bay in Stage-Four Paranoia. I'm a big boy."

"No, you're naked is what you are, and you're not coming back in our boat, because you're creeping me out. I don't like you, and I don't like what you're proposing."

"I can't believe you're naked," Sloane said, covering her eyes and ears. "You are so disgusting."

Mike turned the boat around while Greg led us back to the beach.

"These are great mushrooms, Chelsea. This has probably been one of the best nights of my life."

"Well, it's been the worst of mine," Sloane told him. "I'm telling Mom and Dad."

"Telling them what, Sloane?" Mike asked, clearly annoyed. "No one is smart in this story. Everyone in this scenario is wrong. You're an asshole, I'm a *real* asshole for being a party to this nonsense, Greg is obviously out of his mind, and Chelsea is about two Saturday nights away from being Anna Nicole Smith."

"I'm not wrong," Sloane declared. "I was trying to help my sister save my brother's life."

"Oh, shut up, Sloane," I told her. "At least *we're* on mushrooms. What's *your* excuse?"

Everyone was wiped out except for Greg, who was humming the whole way back to our beach. I felt like I had competed in some sort of Ironman competition and came in after the last person. I hadn't experienced this kind of exhaustion since I'd auditioned for a Nike commercial where they asked me on the spot to choreograph my own workout routine, then promptly suggested that I take ballroom dancing classes at the Learning Annex.

By the time we reached land, my pupils felt like they were going to pop out of my eyes and walk back home alone. We returned the dinghy to its original place, minus one oar, and we all trudged deliriously up to the house.

When we finally walked into the kitchen, the clock said 2:12 A.M. Ray was asleep on the couch we last saw him on, with the television still blaring and a fan about six inches from his face. He looked up when we shut the door, looked at his watch, and looked at us all standing there like rape victims. Then he rolled over and went back to sleep.

I woke up the next day around eleven and went downstairs. My father and Ray were both at the kitchen table discussing how embarrassing the Mets were and if in fact the two of them should change teams.

"Where is everyone?" I asked.

"Oh, everyone left to go swim across to Chappy to see if Greg drowned again," Ray said, shaking his head. "You're worse than the Mets."

My father looked up from the paper. "*Who's* worse than the Mets?"

Greg walked in from outside and planted himself at the kitchen counter, where he began to prepare himself a turkey sandwich. Then he took out a tub of coleslaw from the fridge and set it down between his half-made sandwich and the blender. "Chelsea," he asked as he darted back and forth between the coleslaw and the blender, "can I interest you in a coleslaw smoothie?"

My father took off his glasses. "A coleslaw smoothie? I'll try one of those."

Greg flashed me a big smile while I frowned at him in disgust. "Is there something on your mind, Chelsea?" he asked.

"Yes," I told him, stuffing a half-eaten blueberry pancake into my mouth. "I'm thinking of a two-word phrase. It starts with an 'F' and ends with an 'F.'"

Ray looked up from the table. "Would you like to buy a vowel?"

My brother Greg

Chapter Seven

Black-on-Black Crime

When I travel to New York, I hire a big, black, British driver named Sylvan. I call him Chocolate Chunk. At the end of my trip, he always buys me a little gift and gives it to me when he drops me off at the airport. Last time I left New York, he handed me a small brown paper bag, and once I boarded the plane and was comfortably seated, I opened the paper bag to find a note that read, *This is so that you'll have me with you wherever you're driving. XO, Sylvan.* Attached to it was a key chain that held a minature hairy black gorilla.

Sylvan is a single father who worked his whole life to raise two children in the Bronx and then send them off to college. He is close to three hundred pounds, with a belly that looks like he's in his twelfth month of pregnancy and an ass the size of a Smart Car. After much evaluation I had concluded it was time to get Sylvan some penetration. Since I was not willing to volunteer my own coslopus, I decided to bring him on vacation to Turks and Caicos.

Ted was thrown for a little loop-de-loop when I listed the people who would be accompanying us on our journey to the Caribbean: our gay friend Brian, Paul, Steph, my brother Ray, and Sylvan.

"Sylvan isn't coming."

"Yes, Sylvan is coming."

"Are you being serious?"

"That's correct, and if you bring forth any more questions regarding the matter, I'll also bring Chuy."

"But why?"

"Because Sylvan is one big chocolate chunk nugget, and he needs a vacation."

"If Sylvan were a hundred pounds thinner, you wouldn't ever even have given him the time of day."

"What's your point, Ted? Am I only supposed to give the time of day to people who have their weight under control? If someone asks me what time it is, I'm going to give it to them. Are you asking if I'd be more likely to give it to a fat person? The answer is yes."

He shoved a Ruffles Light potato chip into his mouth. "So let me get this straight. Because of his unregulated diet of Cheetos, apple fritters, and Hawaiian Punch, Sylvan is going to be rewarded with a trip to Turks and Caicos?"

"Now you're catching on. Good work, Detective."

"Well, why don't you charter him a private plane while you're at it?"

"Because *that* would be ridiculous."

"Chelsea, why do you always have to bring random people on vacation with us? This is my vacation, too, remember?"

"Oh, please!" I wailed. I had hit a wall and was weary of being persecuted for trying to do something nice for a fat friend. "You are living the high life! Your whole life is a vacation. I toil my blood, sweat, and tears every day on this silly TV show for your silly network, and then I get on a plane every weekend to fly to some godforsaken city to perform stand-up, and on top of that I have to write another one of these stupid books!" By this point I was clutching my chest like Scarlett in a scene out of *Gone with the Wind*. "And what do you do? You sit around in an office all day, and the biggest decision you have to make is deciding whether or not one of the Kardashians should go full term on one of their pregnancies!"

"All right, Chelsea, would you just calm down already?" he said with a flutter of his chip, walking out of the room. "Go take a laxative or something."

"I'll go away with Sylvan by myself!" I bellowed.

He reappeared in the living room. "You *would* go away with Sylvan alone by yourself. You would do it just to be funny. You would think that's *hilarious*."

"You're absolutely right, Ted," I told him, contemplating the idea. "If I were you, I'd watch yourself."

"Can I just ask you one thing? Why can't we ever go on vacation alone for once, Chelsea? You, me, and Eva?"

"Don't worry. Eva's coming too. I forgot to mention her."

Eva is basically my consigliere and travels with me everywhere I go, because she has her shit together and I do not. I prefer to travel like a white rapper, with many people in tow, and Eva makes this possible. Eva thinks of things no one who wasn't a little insane would think of. She carries a plastic rolling travel bag that holds everything from Q-tips to fat-free cooking spray in three-ounce mini-containers. Once, when Eva, Ted, and I were on a plane from Los Angeles to Miami, I spilled a Bloody Mary, and Eva pulled out some sort of giant paper towel that was absorbent enough to clean up a miscarriage.

"Is that a ShamWow?" Ted exclaimed, spitting his own drink into the seat back ahead of him. "Eva, this is why you're a genius. I just ordered one of those off DR last night."

"Okay, calm down, Ted. What the hell is DR?"

"It's Direct Response, genius. You call 1-800 and they send you stuff."

"No, Ted, *you* call 1-800 and they send you stuff. You, Suzanne Somers, and Ralph Macchio." I put my hand over his mouth and turned to Eva. "Eva, what is that thing?"

"It *is* a ShamWow," she roared, winking at Ted as if he had just put the finishing touches on a Mr. Potato Head. "It's really good for cleaning up messes." Then she got down on her knees and started patting my lap.

"Thank you," I said, grabbing it from her hands. I looked around to see if any other passengers were staring. "You do not have to wipe my lap. Please get up." The problem with Eva is that she insists on doing all the little menial things for me, and when you tell her she doesn't need to, it becomes a discussion, so it's easier to let her just do it in the first place.

Ted loves Eva and thinks her doing things like unpacking my underwear or carrying around five different types of Lean Pockets in her purse is acceptable. He has been a CEO for years and is used to people fawning all over him. He sees nothing wrong with calling his assistant at nine o'clock on a Saturday morning in L.A. to ask her what the weather is like in Rio de Janeiro. Between Eva and Ted, my uselessness had hit an all-time high; there's a strong chance that at this point in my life I wouldn't be able to defrost an ice cube.

"The problem, Ted," I would tell him, "is that I think she might hide a body if I asked her to."

"*That's* the kind of person you want working for you, Chelsea."

I met Eva in Denver at a comedy club and harassed her until she agreed to move to Los Angeles and work on my show. When she first came, she stayed with Ted and me for a couple of months until she found her own place, at which point Ted attempted to convince her to move in with us permanently.

"No fucking way," I told him. "I'm already living

through this hell—there's no way I am going to allow another person to give up her freedom, too."

Eva and Sylvan have always had a special bond, and it grew even more special on our first day on Turks and Caicos, when, during a boat charter, the group jumped into the water and Eva was the first person to realize that Sylvan couldn't swim. Paul, who stayed on board like me, was focused on photographing Stephanie trying to avoid getting her cigarettes wet.

"Aw, fuck!" I said, looking at Sylvan sinking in the water. I ran and got a life ring and threw it at him. Eva swam over to him and grabbed his bear claw of a hand to try to drag him the three feet to the boat's stepladder, but he was flailing his arms and, in a panic, tossed the life ring away from him. I hadn't seen a look of fear this intense since I tried to squeeze Chuy into my compost bin.

"Sylvan, swim!" Steph yelled from a few feet away, waving one hand while the other held her lit American Spirit.

"Don't panic, Sylvan," Eva said calmly as she struggled to keep one side of her face afloat while the other side was being submerged under Sylvan's head, which can weigh eleven to thirteen pounds, depending on how many times he's gone to the bathroom that week.

With Eva's help, Sylvan was able to clutch the bottom of the ladder, where he sat panting. Ted was putting on his flippers and snorkel mask, unaware of the entire episode because his earphones were in.

We had stopped the boat right there when the captain

138

had spotted a dolphin. Luckily for Chocolate Chunk, instead of acting impulsively, I grabbed the dolphin net I'd brought from California and was able to secure it around Sylvan's head.

Paul handed Sylvan a Pellegrino and took a picture of him drinking it. "Sylvan, can you swim?" Paul screamed two inches from Sylvan's face. My friend Paul is obsessed with pictures and is constantly documenting anything that takes place, whether people are cooperating or not.

I elbowed Paul in the ribs and whispered for him to shut his trap. The truth was that it *was* a good question. But the answer was obviously no. If at some point Sylvan had known how to swim, he certainly wasn't able to connect the dots now. Why he would jump into the middle of the ocean and all of a sudden start swimming *was* a little questionable. It was possilble that Sylvan had spent so much time driving on land that maybe he forgot there was a different format for the ocean. In any case, he was clearly embarrassed, and I just wanted him safely back on deck, or in the shallow end of any pool.

This turn of events was a huge blow to me, as I saw this trip as the perfect opportunity to capture some uncommon sea life for our new aquarium. My original idea was to fill it with Maine lobsters and some Chilean sea bass; when we had people over for dinner, they could just spear what they wanted from the tank and everything would be fresh like at Red Lobster. Ted vetoed this idea for some Health Department code that I'm sure he made up, and that's when I came up with my airtight plan to house a single dolphin. The very mention of dolphin fostering sparked a huge debate between Ted and me about the difference between a fish and a water mammal. His argument was that there was no point in lodging a fish if it was something that could survive on land.

"No fish can survive on land," I informed him. "They're called fish because they live in the fucking sea. Unless a lobster hops out of the Long Island Sound and porks a chimpanzee at a zoo in Florida, there is never going to be a fish that survives on land. You got that, Captain Stubing?"

After many vigorous debates and much lengthy consideration, I emerged victorious when Ted finally agreed to a single dolphin on the condition that I do not get it from a vendor but have to capture it myself.

I knew that Ted thought he had put one over on me by making such a demand, but not one to ever underestimate myself, I made contact with several employees at the Atlantis in Bahamas, as well as the VP of marketing at StarKist and was piece by piece putting together a dolphin-abduction strategy.

Once we got to the beach where we were having our lunch, the captain of the boat pulled up nice and close to the shore so Sylvan could walk out. Eva and Steph spent the next three hours giving Sylvan swimming lessons while Paul forked over the $150 he bet me that Sylvan was never coming to Turks and Caicos in the first place.

"Is this one of her jokes?" Paul asked Ted when we all got to the island. "Is Sylvan really coming?"

"I don't know, maybe. I think he's coming, but I don't even know what's real and what isn't anymore. Three weeks ago she convinced me that it was legal to have an alligator dwell with you as long as you create a swamplike environment in a spare bedroom."

"Well, Ted, that is a little ridiculous. Why would you believe that?"

"Because she had the story so perfectly ironed out *and* she had convinced me there were alligator animal shelters, which I still think might be true."

"I think that *might* actually be true," my brother Ray said.

"Neither is true, you idiots," I chimed in.

By this point Ted's reality had become so warped he didn't even know what was reality and what was fantasy. I felt good about my position in the world, and I felt even better that I had developed so much mistrust among my close friends that they were constantly confused and disoriented.

The truth of the matter was this: I wanted Sylvan to experience the kind of vacation that in recent years I had become lucky enough to afford. *Of course* penetration was at the forefront of my mind, but I've learned through previous experiences that while trying to get someone else penetrated is ultimately an altruistic endeavor, it can be exhausting and, more often than not, fruitless. By the end of the week, I had given up my sexual aspirations for him and focused on enjoying our time together and, more important, enjoying the splendor of watching his Chocolate Chunk mess of a body wade around like a rhinoceros in a one-piece.

"I love you, Sylvan," I'd tell him as I swam into his arms and held on to his tits.

"I love you, too, Chels."

On our very last day on the island, we were all sitting in the lounge area of the pool when Steph noticed two Mocha Mamas sipping on mai tais. They were a little drunk, and Stephanie was very drunk, seeing as she hadn't left the pool bar for seven hours and was now chain-smoking while simultaneously making arrangements to move in with the Filipino bartender, who had casually mentioned that he always wanted to visit Los Angeles, more specifically, the La Brea Tar Pits.

Steph and I swam over and said hello to her new friends Feliqua and Wendy.

"You look familiar," Feliqua told me, and Wendy nodded in agreement. "Are you that lady on the TV? Tracy Lately?"

"That's right," I said, and then took Stephanie's lit cigarette from her hand and put it out in her drink while she was focusing her attention on our new friends. "Steph, did you tell the ladies about the dolphin we saw snorkeling and how you were unable to submerge your head underwater because you refused to put out your American Spirit?"

Paul swam up right behind me. "Stephanie! I didn't know you smoked!"

Stephanie ignored Paul and started looking for her cigarette. Feliqua announced that it was her fortieth-birthday celebration. She then led us in a very special rendition of "Happy Birthday" to herself, and afterward, Steph and Brian interrogated both of the ladies about what kind of men they were into. By this time the women had nicknamed Brian "Delicious" because he's gay, from the South, and has two basketballs for an ass that sit about a half inch under his shoulders.

Brian is originally from Atlanta and enjoys nothing more than black people from the South, but his true passion lies in the old sitcom *Designing Women*. He's an author who's very handsome and athletic, and he once spent an afternoon trying to convince me to executive-produce an updated, modern-day version of *Designing Women*, but with four gay guys. When I reminded him that someone already did that show and it was called *Queer Eye for the Straight Guy*, he guffawed. "What about with four black women?"

"That was *227*."

If you closed your eyes when Delicious laughed, he sounded exactly like Mrs. Garrett. The ladies loved him. Their laughs were just as loud as Delicious's and turned into a booming din as they kept high-fiving each other and screeching with their mouths wide open. The girls worked together as hospital administrators in Nashville, and both were at least at a 1.5 blood-alcohol level.

"You got an ass like a sister," Feliqua kept telling Delicious. Then he'd snuggle up closer to them and squeal, "I found my two Cocoa Sisters! Ahahahahahahh!"

Feliqua looked a lot like Whoopi Goldberg and kept asking us if we saw the resemblance. It was clear that she was not happy about this comparison, so we all shook our heads in unison and said, "No fucking way," every time she asked.

"I've met Whoopi," I reassured her. "Unless you're wearing Crocs under that water, you have very little in common."

Their nachos and conch fritters were delivered to the swim-up bar, along with the food the rest of us had ordered. When I sat down next to Feliqua, she looked at my salad and then looked at me. "What's the matter, Tracy Lately? You one of those skinny bitches can't eat no french fries, can't eat no grits?"

"I can eat," I told her. "I could probably eat your ass under the table, but I prefer to drink my nourishment when I'm on vacation, and this right here's a blended passionfruit margarita, no salt. Would you like to try it, Fatwa?"

"If it's free, you bet your ass I'm gonna try it," she declared, right before she grabbed it out of my hand and captured my straw with her tongue.

"Tracy Lately! Ahahhahahahh! I love it!" Delicious was now screaming and started jumping up and down in the water, splashing himself. "The Tasty Cocoa Sisters are ready to part-ee with Tracy Lately!"

Stephanie splashed water on the back of my head, and when I turned around, she exhaled a billow of smoke into my face. "They're single . . . and horny! Where is Chocolate Chunk?"

"Where is Sylvan?" I turned to Paul, who was busy taking pictures of Wendy and Feliqua making a sandwich with Delicious.

"I don't know where Sylvan is, Tracy," Paul answered, "but I hope he's not in the fucking ocean."

I looked over to find Eva arranging all of our flip-flops by the edge of the pool. "Eva." I jerked my head in the direction of the ladies. "Get Sylvan."

"Ray is giving him a swimming lesson on the beach! Why don't we all go down to the ocean?" She winked at me. My brother Ray was in no position to be giving anyone a swimming lesson, considering he had nearly drowned swimming up to the pool bar earlier, but I was more alarmed that Eva couldn't control her winking. I thought I had clarified with her that winking was for rappers and cougars, but for some reason it was her go-to move, and our conversations to the contrary didn't seem to be having an effect.

"That's a great idea," Stephanie said, grabbing her cigarettes. "Ladies, would you like to meet Sylvan? He's a real cutie, but he's very shy."

"Shit, can we bring our drinks?" asked Wendy.

"You bet," Paul told them. "I'll carry them—and I'll bring your food."

There was excitement in the air, and it was impossible not to feel the energy. I ran ahead of the group to tell the others that the ocean was about to get some new company. Ray was giving very specific instructions to Sylvan on how to float facedown, while Ted was fifty feet out swimming back and forth with his usual snorkel equipment. I quickly briefed Sylvan and told him to stand up, stand tall, and act proud. We turned to face the resort when we heard raucous laughter and felt what seemed like tectonic plates shifting. Wendy and Feliqua were running full steam ahead into the ocean with their drinks still in their hands and spilling all over the beach. Paul was doing the same with nachos and conch fritters while simultaneously taking action shots.

"Holy shit," Ray said, backing into the ocean. "Are they coming for us?"

After I watched Wendy and Feliqua barrel into the surf like two bulldozers, it became apparent that Sylvan wasn't the only black person who couldn't swim.

"Oh, my God!" Paul screamed, running in after them with two water noodles in his hand. "Why can't anyone swim?"

The women were screaming and laughing and swallowing water. They kept trying to regain their footing but continually fell down until Delicious and Sylvan were able to balance each one. Sylvan made it over to Wendy to lend her a hand, but when she felt a touch, she turned around and spit in his face.

"Aaaaaahhhahahahahahhahahh!!!" was the only sound anyone heard from Delicious.

"I'm sorry," she slurred, wiping the spit off Sylvan's face. "I thought you were the beach." Then she turned in the other direction and hawked another loogie, which the wind blew right back into her face. She quickly fell in the water, but Sylvan grabbed her.

"My weave! My weave!" Wendy yelled when she was done spitting.

"I got you, girl," Sylvan told her.

"I lost two tracks yesterday when we went swimming. Everyone at church told me not to go in the ocean. You'll lose your weave in a hot second!" Then she smacked Sylvan on the ass and went flying into one of Stephanie's lit cigarettes.

"Do you really need to smoke in the ocean?" I asked her for the third time that week.

"Stephanie, I didn't know you smoked," Paul said, then started howling along with Delicious, who was still moaning with laughter while holding Feliqua like a baby in the water.

"Aaaahhahahhahahahahahahahh!"

My brother had commandeered one of the water noodles and was using it to defend himself from all the splashing. "Chelsea, can you believe Sylvan went from not knowing how to swim to rescuing people in one week? I should probably look into coaching some sort of black swim team."

"They're standing in two feet of water, Ray. Even though a black swim team does seem like an oxymoron at this point, it is definitely something to think about. In the winter you could teach interracial skiing."

Feliqua, who was definitely more drunk than Wendy, tried to sit in the shallow water, but small waves kept pushing her back on the beach. She had no upper-body control, so Paul helped her to the edge of the beach, where she retrieved her drink and lay down on Paul's lap.

"We got a Cocoa Sister down. One Cocoa Sister down!" Paul yelled to us as he took a picture of himself smiling with her.

"I didn't know there were gay traffic controllers that also lifeguarded," Ray said to Paul after he walked up to have a sip of Feliqua's cocktail. "It's okay, Feliqua. We'll take care of you."

She announced she needed a nap and fell asleep on Paul's lap. Two minutes later she was awake again and calling for Wendy.

Wendy stormed over to me and asked me where Sylvan was. "Right behind you," I told her.

"You shut up, you white skinny TV bitch. You know you need a bodyguard for that non-french-fry-eating ass." She followed this up with a smack to my ass and asked me to check her weave, which I straightened. Then I took one side of the back of her bathing suit and pulled it into the crack of her ass, where she left it.

"Black don't crack, you silly bitch!" Then she fell into

the water and came back up for another round of apple bobbing.

"Get together for a picture!" Paul screamed to me and Wendy, who had already somehow made her way back to Sylvan and was mounting him.

"Honey, I need you to take care of me. They said you're a good man and a single father. I can't really swim. Hold me, Sylvan."

"Happy birthday, Feliqua!" Paul screamed into Feliqua's face, and then adjusted her weave. "Is this thing reversible?"

Delicious was now howling so hard he was literally choking on the ocean, but no one seemed to care.

Sylvan and Wendy were drifting farther away from us but managing to keep in water shallow enough to stay afloat. And then I heard him say, "Are you sure we're not being obvious?"

When I looked over, Sylvan was behind Wendy and moving like a jackrabbit while her head was bobbing back and forth and her weave was whipping him in the face. "Shhhh!" she told him. "For all those white folks know, we snorkeling. Give it to me!"

"I think Daddy's coming home," Ray announced as he got back out of the water. "I'm getting my camera."

"Oh, my God, you should see all the fish out there," I heard behind me, and turned around to see Ted standing there with his snorkel mask and goggles still on.

"I don't think so, buddy," I told him. "I got a couple of

bigger fish, and a lot of things have happened while you were discovering marine life."

Once he surveyed the scene and was able to compute what was taking place, he put his snorkel and mask on again, turned around, and headed back out to sea.

Feliqua got up from her seat in the sand next to Paul and said she needed to go lie down. Delicious and I got out of the ocean and guided her to one of the chaise longues closest to the beach. "Delicious," she moaned. "Can you get me a ginger ale?"

Brian went to get the ginger ale while I sat down and coached her on how to projectile-vomit into the sand.

"Get it out, Fataqua," my brother said as he neared us. He had a towel in his hand and leaned over to wipe her mouth and then looked at me. "Who the fuck is Delicious?"

"Brian," I told him.

"I need ginger ale!"

"It's coming, Feliqua," I told her.

"So am I!" she moaned, and threw up again.

When I turned to go back into the water, Sylvan and Wendy were heading toward us, with Wendy very unstable on her feet. The sand was not her friend, and Sylvan was having trouble keeping them both upright at the same time. She stopped halfway to the lounge chairs and turned around to face the ocean. She pulled the back of her bathing suit in between her ass cheeks and started shaking her ass.

"Aaaahhahahahahahahhh," shrieked Delicious again.

"Oh, my Lord," Sylvan said, taking a step back and looking at me. "People wonder how the Caribbean was formed, Chels, and now I know. A black woman shook her ass, and a bunch of islands were created as aftershocks."

Paul instructed them to both bend over for a snapshot.

Wendy lost her footing. She didn't fall on her ass, which would be the obvious gravitational pull—probably for the entire island—but face-first, a header straight into the sand. Sylvan went down after her but managed to land on his side. Paul was the first on the scene with his camera in tow, and what he captured has been seen only in *National Geographic*. Two chocolate sand dabs, washed ashore.

There was sand in every crevice of Wendy's face. Her eyes, her ears, her nose. Brian grabbed one of the ginger ales that he'd brought for Feliqua and poured it over Wendy's head. "We're going to need a two-liter, Brian," Ray told him. "Sorry, I mean Delicious."

Ted had reappeared from the ocean and was running toward us yelling, "Oh, my God! Is she dead? Wait, keep her alive. I know CPR."

That was all Wendy needed to get her groove back. She was howling harder than any of us, but the sand was still pissed.

She was attempting to spit out some of the sand when we all played Light as a Feather, Stiff as a Board and carried her back into the ocean, where she could properly rinse off. Stephanie, of course, could assist with only one hand.

"Aren't you out of cigarettes yet?" I asked her.

"Stephanie, I didn't know you smoked!"

"Paul, shut up!" everyone yelled at the same time.

As luck would have it, the dip in the ocean was exactly what the doctor ordered for Wendy, because after that she was at least able to manage her footsteps in a more reasonable manner. We all sat in the water, exhausted, for a good hour before it started to get dark out, but Feliqua was not anywhere close to moving. She had stopped throwing up, sort of, but was firm about staying where she was. "Don't fucking touch me!" she yelled. Wendy said she needed help getting Feliqua to her room, and then she would be available to have dinner with us.

Sylvan volunteered to stay with the girls, and Stephanie announced that she had only two cigarettes left.

"It might be time to give it a rest, Steph," Paul told her. "Your breath is like eighty proof."

Stephanie walked off in a huff, and Eva followed her. Ray was floating on the noodles, watching everything from the water. Ted nudged me and said he'd like to talk to me privately. "In the ocean, please."

Once we were back in the water, Ray took two water noodles out from under him and handed them to us. "What an amazing day. I taught a man how to swim, and he took that knowledge and saved another person. I don't think I've ever felt more alive."

"That's fantastic, Ray," Ted told him, and then turned to me. "We need to discuss dinner. Are these women joining us?"

"I don't think Feliqua is having dinner tonight, Ted, but Wendy doesn't look like she misses many meals."

"Oh, my God!" exclaimed Steph. "Oh, my God!"

I looked back and saw Delicious, Paul, and Sylvan wheeling Feliqua on a chaise longue away from the beach up to the pool area. "I'll be back for dinner!" Wendy yelled over her shoulder as she mounted the steps to the hotel. The three of us ran out of the water and followed them.

"What are you doing?" Ted yelled. "Are you taking her to her room?"

"We're not fucking staying here. We heard there was a swim-up bar. Our hotel's down the beach!" Wendy told Ted. "You better put on your dancing shoes. I hear you move like Michael Jackson."

Boom was the sound the lounge chair made every time it hit a step.

Feliqua would groan a little each time. "Ow."

"This is some crazy shit," Wendy announced. "You white people are CUH-razy."

After getting Feliqua up the stairs, we had to pass the pool area, which to our surprise was holding a screening of *Pirates of the Caribbean*. Delicious and Sylvan put on their happy faces as they strolled through various couples watching a movie over a candlelight dinner.

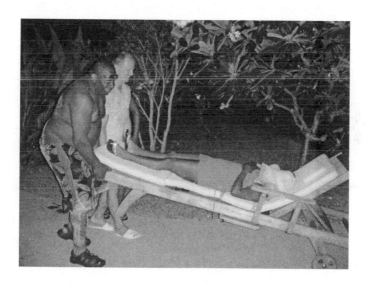

"You guys," I whispered. "We can't wheel a black woman through a movie screening in a chaise longue. There's got to be some sort of law against that."

"We've got to get our girl into a taxi, Tracy. Chunky Chocolate is going to ride back with me to drop off my girl, and then I'll be heading back for that barbecue. Yeah, yeah, yeah. A girl's gotta eat. I swam the shit out of that ocean today!"

There was no point in trying to make less of a scene than we were already making, as we were in full view of all the moviegoers. We just kept our heads down while we pushed a person in a chaise longue along the path in our bathing suits. I volunteered for Feliqua to sleep in Sylvan's room until I looked at Sylvan, who wasn't smiling. At least it looked like he wasn't smiling; it might have been too dark to tell.

A security guard came running over to us and handed me a bathrobe. "Mrs. Handler? Can we be of some help?" That's when Ted decided to make a quick left and go up to our room.

"We're good, thanks," I reassured him. "We're playing hide-and-seek. She's just pretending to be asleep." Wendy and I walked on either side of the chaise longue in order to stop Feliqua from falling onto the concrete. Paul was following closely behind, vacillating between picture mode and video mode. There was clearly too much footage to capture for any documentarian. We had to make sudden, corrective moves every time we hit a set of stairs or a proverbial speed bump, which would result in more grunts from Feliqua.

"This is the best fucking night of my life," Wendy shouted. "I think I might pee myself. Sylvan, you're gonna come with us in the taxi, right, motherfucker?"

"Aahhahahahahahahhhh!"

"Brian, do you need me to give you the Heimlich?" I asked him.

"It's fucking Delicious, Tracy!" Wendy corrected me.

"Baby, I ain't gonna let nothing happen to you or Feliqua," Sylvan told her. "I'll come back to your hotel and make sure you are safe."

"Damn, you motherfuckers know how to party!" Wendy screamed. "Especially you, white bitch! I'm 'bout ready to piss myself!"

"You think you're going to pee yourself?" I snapped back at her. "Do you have any idea what condition I'm dealing with? I can't take much more of this. We just wheeled a person in a wheelbarrow off a beach, through a movie screening, and on our way to a lobby."

Feliqua grumbled again, and Delicious asked if she was okay. "It's too bumpy," she slurred.

Wendy was Feliqua's closest kin and had made it clear she would be speaking for her until Feliqua came back to life. "She's gonna be fine if this little anorexic bitch would stop her bitchin' and enjoy the beautiful night." I guess Wendy wanted to show me some affection, because her next move was to shoulder-check me into the bushes,

which turned out to be a fitting place to relieve myself.
When I was done, I rolled over and lay on the sidewalk
while Paul took pictures of me in my own puddle.

Once he got the shot he needed, he moved on to the
matter at hand or, as he described it, "to see the girls out."

"Bye!" I yelled after them. "Bye, girls!"

"Oh, I'll be back, shitface!" Wendy hollered.

The next day Sylvan had an early flight, so I didn't get to
see him before he left, but he sent me a text saying that he
wanted me to know he never had sex with Wendy and that
he only got dry-humped by her: "please trust that she was
the aggressor, chelz. I did get to see her booty which was
nice and big, like a full moon."

I showed the text to Ted after I stopped convulsing.

"Oh, my God. He's worried you're upset? Little does
he know, this is what you live for. That's the main difference between you and me, Chelsea. I consider last night a
mockery. You consider last night one of the best nights of
your life and a huge success."

"Maybe I do."

"I've never seen anything like that in all my life."

"Well, you've obviously been running with the wrong
crowd. It was like God came down from the sky and
handed me an Easter basket. An Easter basket with three
chocolate bunnies."

I turned sideways in bed to face Ted. "Did I ever tell
you that my favorite holiday used to be Black Friday?"

Since I have one African-American friend, when I found out about this holiday, I thought: It's about time. I was psyched that she would have a day just to relax and celebrate herself for being black. I also thought it was really nice that Black Friday took place the day after Thanksgiving; if my friend worked for someone who didn't take advantage and give her a four-day weekend, she could still get off work by telling her boss that she's black and Friday was her day. I had forgotten to get my friend Loni a gift for Black Friday a couple of years ago, so I ran to the mall to get her a new weave. The place was a disaster; all the stores were having sales and there were people everywhere. That's when I found out what Black Friday was. I've since turned my attention to Flag Day, primarily because I'm a fan of June.

"That's a pretty dumb story," Ted declared, when I was done.

"Thank you," I replied. "I appreciate you taking the time to listen."

Chapter Eight

Dear Asshole

Against all good and reasonable judgment, my men-
tally retarded father insists on renting his Martha's
Vineyard summer home at astronomical rates, mostly based
on how much income he perceives the family who's renting makes. His assessment depends on three factors: their
vocabulary during the initial phone conversation, the region
of the country they live in, and how much experience he
thinks they have in being taken advantage of.

The following is an e-mail my sister Sloane forwarded
me from one of my father's renters after the renter and her
family made the mistake of paying to stay at our house.

July 16, 2008

This is a lovely letter from last week's renters. They came after dad stayed for 1 week and chose NOT to have maid service after his stay or attempt to clean up after himself AT ALL before leaving the house. He is cagey about who he brought to the vineyard with him which means it was one of his Jamaican girlfriends...enjoy.

July 14, 2008

Mr. Melvin Handler
35 Morningside Drive
Livingston, NJ 07039

Dear Mr. Handler,

This letter is intended to follow up in writing on the telephone conversation that you had with my husband, on Tuesday morning, July 8, 2008. During that conversation, my husband detailed to you a number of problems and deficiencies that we discovered on July 6th and 7th upon our arrival at your home on Martha's Vineyard, for which we had contracted a week's rental from July 6–13, 2008 for the price of $7,900, including a $150 housekeeping fee, plus a $500 security deposit.

Our initial realization upon our arrival was that the house had not been cleaned. There was food left out on the counter, in the cupboards and in the refrigerator and freezer, most of which was well past usable condition. The counter, stovetop, toaster and table were covered with crumbs and food stains; the oven and refrigerator shelves were very dirty. Someone had left a package of squid (bait?) behind in the freezer, which had melted (due to freezer problems described below) and dripped smelly, fishy puddles onto the bottom of the freezer unit. We all spent the first several hours in our "vacation home" cleaning the kitchen and bathrooms and sweeping floors. As you might imagine, that was hardly the way we had hoped to begin our stay on Martha's Vineyard.

Also, the grill was filthy to the point of being unusable. My husband went out and purchased tools to clean it, and he and a friend (that hasn't spoken to us since) spent several hours scrubbing grilling racks, burners and the inside of the grill to remove grease and food debris, and hosing it down before we could reasonably cook on it. By this time, one of our other friends had already gone to the local hardware store and purchased a new grill for $479.95 which we had shipped back to our house in West Virginia at the end of our week for another $275.00.

Additionally, we found that items that we assumed belonged to your family had not been removed or stored prior to our visit. There were clothes in closets and drawers, along with children's toys and boogie boards and home maintenance items such as paint [and] varnish cans. There was a full laundry basket of unfolded towels and dirty clothes in the laundry room, as well as dozens of household items stored untidily under the kitchen sink and in the laundry room, not to mention an empty container of Tide cleaning detergent.

As our first 24 hours in the house progressed, we realized that there were several essential appliances that simply did not work, including:

• the refrigerator and freezer. While we were able to maintain the refrigerator portion somewhat cool by turning the cooling dial to its maximum level, the freezer did not work at all.

• the dishwasher. We loaded it to capacity Sunday night and Monday morning after our initial meals, added detergent and set it to run when we left for the beach Monday morning. Upon our return seven hours later, the dishwasher was still running. We had to unload the dishwasher and wash all of the dishes, which were caked with dried soap.

• the toaster. The manual "pop-up" latch was broken, which required two of us to jury-rig a method for getting the toast out before it overcooked by turning down the "light/dark" knob and pulling forcefully up on the toasting lever. My husband and I sustained several small burns on our fore and middle fingers, since we were too embarrassed to let anyone else use the toaster.

Additionally, there were several areas of the house in serious need of repair:

• The ceiling in the first floor bathroom had an obvious plaster patch over the toilet. On Monday evening, that patch fell through, scattering plaster dust and ceiling pieces around the toilet and bathroom floor. Throughout the week, small bits of plaster and drops of water fell into the bathroom.

• The bathtub faucet in the first floor bathroom leaked a continuous stream of very hot water into the tub and had corroded right through the faucet itself. Both the tub and faucet were rusted badly. We came to the determination that this constant hot water leak must have been a contributing factor to the complete shortage of hot water for showers; when ten of us returned from the beach and wanted to clean up, only two of us could do so with even reasonably warm water.

• While there were three screen doors out onto the deck and one in each of the first floor bedrooms, one screen door in the living room was completely blocked by the location of the television set, while the other two, as well as the one from the bedroom to the back deck, came off in our hands upon our first exit from the house. We set them back on their tracks, but were forced to "repair" them constantly throughout the week in order to use the deck at all.

• One of the benches to the outdoor picnic table was split through. We did not use it for obvious safety reasons. Having to drag kitchen chairs outside in order to be able to eat as a group outside was a huge inconvenience.

• The "downstairs apartment" was a disaster. Not only did we feel that it was seriously misrepresented (detailed below), it was musty and buggy. The dehumidifier which was running down there was clearly inadequate, and the decision to run the dehumidifier hose into the downstairs shower stall made the shower dirty and unusable.

Finally, we felt that there were some serious misrepresentations in both your online description of the house, and in the conversations that you and I had prior to our decision to rent the house for the week:

• As mentioned, the basement was a disaster. When you and I spoke, I expressed reservations about bedrooms in "a basement." Your response was (which I wrote down at the time to pass on to our friends involved in the rental with us) "It's not so much a basement as a first floor and it also has a separate entrance." Mr. Handler, an underground room with no windows is definitely what I would consider to be a "basement." While furnished comfortably, the downstairs rooms were dark and dank, very musty and extremely buggy. Your response when my husband expressed concerns on the telephone about the mustiness in the basement was to prop open the outside door for a few hours; that resulted in even more bugs, as well as unraked leaves being blown in all over the floor. Having to spray our children with bug spray from head to toe in order for them to go to bed seems more than ridiculous; having to shake all of their clothing, towels and bedding to remove spiders and earwigs before packing to go home is outrageous.

- Also, never did we imagine that the "separate entrance" was the ONLY entrance to that floor. Even an actual basement can usually be accessed from inside the house. That said, if there were only an external entrance, one might expect lights on the path or at the door to facilitate going downstairs in the dark. We necessarily purchased flashlights for the kids just to help them find their way down there to go to bed.

- The upstairs "queen bedroom" (which has a full-size mattress on the bed, by the way) had no fourth wall or door. As my husband described it, "it was like sleeping in the hallway." We had no privacy and were unable to let the teen-agers stay up late upstairs in the living room to watch TV or play video games because of the openness of that bedroom to the downstairs level.

• We were never sure of the appropriate path to "our beach." There were no clarifying directions at the house and your description on the telephone of using the path "on the left" led us either to your neighbor's gate or a different neighbor's lawn. When we followed the path through the open lawn, we found a beach filled with boats—clearly not a private beach that went with the house. There were several docks there as well (which would have been a better alternative for sitting down at the bay than the small beach next to the wetlands, which was extremely buggy), but we determined them all to belong to other houses.

• Our experience has been that a house intended to "sleep 12" would also provide accommodations to "feed 12." Our intention in renting the house together was to enable us to spend time together and socialize. There was no table or space in the house that would allow us to all eat a meal together. We moved furniture, brought chairs up from the basement and, once again, "jury-rigged" a solution, but it was a huge inconvenience and was a factor, along with the lack of refrigeration, that led to us choosing to eat out much more than we normally would have during our vacation week.

As you might imagine, Mr. Handler, after wading through three pages of complaints and concerns, we were extremely disappointed in our experience in renting your house for our week on Martha's Vineyard. The fact that you were aware of the problem with the dishwasher and didn't inform us in any way, and that we made you aware of the refrigeration issue on Monday and you never contacted us with a repair plan, or at the very least an *apology*, is truly unacceptable. I have no idea how much experience you may have in renting out your home, but we have rented homes all over the Cape and Islands, New England, Florida, California and even in Europe over the past 25 years and have never had to deal with anything close to the inadequacies, misrepresentations and lack of information (trash pick-up?) that we endured last week.

Our original agreement stipulated that you would return the $500 security deposit we paid upon completion of the rental. Considering the fact that we left the house in much better condition than we found it, we would certainly anticipate the refund of that full amount. I would also respectfully request the refund of the $150 housekeeping fee, since there was no evidence of any housekeeping activities occurring prior to our arrival.

Finally, we strongly believe that you owe us a partial refund of the rent that we paid for the week, in compensation for the groceries we had brought with us (dairy products, luncheon meat, freezer items, fruit and vegetables, leftovers, etc.) that were lost due to inadequate refrigeration and freezer capabilities, the groceries that we had to purchase to replace these items and the innumerable bags of ice that were required to keep anything really cold at all. We also feel that a refund is due to compensate us for the huge inconveniences we experienced, from at least daily trips to Stop & Shop to replace food that had gone bad or to purchase for daily meals rather than being able to do one "big shopping," to spending so much time cleaning up after your previous guests, to changing our plans to spend a good share of the day Tuesday dealing with the appliance repair shop. Since we paid $7,750 to rent the house for seven days, we feel that a refund of one full day's rental fee ($1,121 in addition to the $150 housekeeping fee and $500 security deposit) would be the *least* we would expect.

On behalf of your future tenants, I would urge you to pay immediate attention to these items that

I have outlined—there are no families expecting
an idyllic Martha's Vineyard vacation experience
that would find the current conditions of your
home to be acceptable. I also would hope that
you would be more forthcoming on the set-up of
the house and perhaps target smaller groups or
families—the accommodations may be useable for
your own family, but groups paying so dearly for
the privilege of staying in an island home would
expect, and certainly deserve, much more. We were
extremely fortunate with the spectacular weather
last week—I cannot imagine a 12-person group's
experience at your home during a week of rain.

I look forward to receiving a refund check in
the amount of $1,871, as detailed above, from you
as soon as possible.

I picked up the phone and called Sloane. "This letter is
ridiculous," I told her.

"I know, he's so humiliating."

"I can't believe this woman is only asking for her deposit
and a day of the rental fee. Is she retarded?" I asked.

"I don't know, but her friends are probably never going
to speak to her again for renting a house like that in the
first place. She even mentioned it in the letter. Did you see
that part?"

"Yes, I saw that part."

"You know, he tells everyone you're his daughter, and

if they don't know who you are, he pulls out your books or tells them what time your show is on and also when it repeats."

"Oh, my God, I didn't even think of that. What a dick."

"Yup."

"Well then, you have to take down the online ads for the property. He can't continue to rent that house."

"I did, Chelsea!"

"Then how did he rent it? He doesn't know how to get online, and even if he did, his fingers are too fat to use a computer."

"He has some friend who owns a restaurant or something. Mario. I think he helps Dad."

"Who?"

"I don't know, Chelsea. Don't ask. Some weird Italian guy who thinks Dad is hilarious. It's very strange. I think he thinks Dad has money or something. I don't know what's going on there."

"What do you mean, 'what's going on there'? What do you think is going on?"

"Well, nothing sexual, if that's what you're getting at."

"What?"

"I know how your mind works, Chelsea."

"Really, Sloane? You think that I think Dad is sleeping with an Italian man?"

"I don't know."

"Sloane, shut up. I'm asking why Mario would be doing anything for Dad."

"Maybe Mario's the Jamaican cleaning lady's pimp," she speculated. "I have no idea. I tell you I think he thinks Dad has money."

"Who would think Dad has money? He wears house slippers to temple and has hair growing out of his eyes. Not to mention he drives a minivan that looks like the *Rock of Love* bus."

"Chelsea, he tells people about his homes and describes them using words like 'paradise' and 'ecstasy.'"

"Ew."

"If I were you, I would change my last name, because he's got more energy than ever, and I don't think he's going to die anytime soon."

"That's wonderful. Well, he has to reimburse this woman, and not only for her deposit. He needs to give her all her money back."

"He probably already spent it. He just borrowed another five thousand dollars from Ray, after he sat in my living room, ate an entire pizza, and told me *I* looked like I put on a few pounds."

"Oh, my God, what is wrong with you people? Why do you keep giving him money? He's never going to sell the Livingston house if you guys keep loaning him money."

"Ray told him that's the last time. Greg's going over there next week with a Realtor to talk about listing the property. He told Dad he has no money left, and we all have families to raise and that he is cut off monetarily from all of us."

"I'm calling Dad. I'll call you back."

"Don't tell him I e-mailed you that letter, Chelsea. He'll call me and yell at me—or worse, come over. He already has one of his cars in our driveway and is mad at me because I told him it was embarrassing and asked him to move it."

Sloane's kids were both screaming in the background without any reaction from her, so I hung up. I was disgusted with her lack of respect for herself and her driveway. I looked at Ted, who was shaking his head in disgust.

"Has anyone tried to talk to your father about the legal ramifications of renting a house that is in such disrepair?" Ted asked. "I mean, someone could hurt themselves and he could lose the entire property."

"No, Ted, no one has ever said anything to him about it," I said as I smacked the palm of my hand against the side of my forehead. "Of course we've told him! He's a giant fuckwad who thinks the whole world is out to get him. He doesn't listen to anyone, and he is not a reasonable person. We're dealing with a psychopath."

Ted couldn't grasp how my father couldn't be reasoned with. He grew up with parents who paid their bills on time, got their shots on time, and pinned his ears back to the sides of his head when he slept. My parents didn't even care if I *had* ears.

I picked up the phone and dialed my father's number, half hoping it would be disconnected.

"Is that you?" he answered, in the singsongy way he answers the phone every time I call, as if we are about to reminisce about all the amazing days of my childhood when I would get screamed at for not knowing the capital of Hungary.

"Yeah, it's me."

"How ya doing, love? I miss you."

"That's nice, but I just got a letter from one of your Vineyard rentals that is about three pages long detailing everything that was wrong in the house."

"Who?"

"You know who, Dad. A letter from the woman who brought twelve people to the Vineyard and nothing in the house worked." I looked at the letter on my computer. "A Mrs. Danziger."

"Oh, that woman. She needs a psychiatrist."

"No, Dad. *You* need a psychiatrist."

He chuckled at this. "That woman complained about everything. She was a pain in the tuchus when she called me on the phone to rent the property in the first place. I should have known then she was going to cause problems. She's a schoolteacher from West Virginia. West Virginia's got the highest delinquency rate in the country, Chels. Woman is obviously confused."

"Dad, the freezer and the refrigerator did not work. They had melted squid leaking out onto the kitchen floor, and the dishwasher was broken, and that's only the first paragraph."

"Chelsea, that squid I left for them was a welcoming gift. I had some extra left from a little barbecue I threw and thought it would be a nice gesture to leave it for them, and this is the response I get?" He followed that with a loud grunt and a cough that sounded like he was spitting up a chicken wing that had gone down the wrong pipe.

"What was that?"

"A rib, that's all," he declared, and was back to speaking clearly again. I looked at Ted, who was reading the Robb Report, then back at the letter.

"A barbecue you held? Since when do you throw barbecues? I thought you just eat at McDonald's every day."

"That's right."

"What's right?"

"Both are right, but there's no McDonald's on the Vineyard, so I had a couple of friends over."

To be very clear, my father has no friends, so when he says anything intimating that he does, I know more likely than not he is referring to one of his Jamaican girlfriends. None of my brothers and sisters can get an honest answer from him regarding his personal life, and, to be honest, we'd rather not know the details. We just know that he is very secretive, has a prescription for Cialis, and frequently has over young black Jamaican women who are supposedly "cleaning" and hide in the bathroom when someone drops by his house unannounced.

"Who would come to your barbecue?"

"What kind of question is that?" he asked, still in a jocular mood. He was enjoying our little conversation and didn't know it was about to go south fast.

"A pretty good one, if you ask me. You left all the food on the barbecue grill and didn't even clean it when you were done, and since when do you even know how to operate a barbecue, Dad? What are you even talking about?"

"Chelsea, darling, you are in such a *precarious* mood."

"Please don't call me darling. Actually, don't call me Chelsea either."

"Well, what would you suggest I call you, then?"

"Who were you up there with, and why didn't you have your little cleaning-lady girlfriend clean up your mess before you left?"

"I don't know what you're referring to, love, but I told the maids to come before I left, so if they didn't, then obviously they're unreliable. I don't see how I'm at fault."

I could tell from the inflection in his voice that he wasn't comprehending the seriousness of my mood. This had happened throughout my childhood, but with the roles reversed, with him chasing after me with whatever food item was closest to him.

"Listen up, fathead." I wanted to get to the point of the phone call and had to make up something that would force him to reimburse this woman's funds. "I just got a call from the *Martha's Vineyard Times*, and guess what they said?"

"What?"

"They said they're writing a story about the fact that Chelsea Handler's father, who owns property on the Vineyard, is misrepresenting his home to renters, even after several complaints that have been ignored by you, and they have the woman's letter, which they are planning on printing in full."

"Who called?" The lilt in his voice was replaced with a crack and a shot of adrenaline.

"A reporter from the *Martha's Vineyard Times*, Dad. You are not allowed to misrepresent a property, not clean it, have no appliances working when they get there, broken screen doors, and a cellar that you try to pass off as a bungalow. Are you out of your mind?"

"How did they get the letter?"

"I'm assuming Mrs. Danziger sent it to them in her state of fury. If she doesn't receive her refund by this Friday, they are going to print it in Sunday's edition. You'll never be able to rent again, and you're now dragging my name through the mud with yours." Ted was looking at me while he opened the *L.A. Times*.

"The woman is an extortionist. I told her my daughter was a best-selling author and a movie star. She obviously watched your show and saw an opportunity."

"No, Dad. Staying at your house is not an opportunity. It's the opposite of an opportunity. It is a sentence. You screwed this woman over, and she is pissed, as she should be. And furthermore, why did you even mention my name? Why would you do that? And by the way, I'm not a movie star. I'm on cable."

"Because you are my daughter and your daddy is very proud of you."

"That's nice, Dad, but *I'm* not proud of *you*. You treat people like garbage, and this woman probably saved up all year to go on what she thought was going to be a beautiful vacation, and she shows up to melted fish on the floor and a filthy house filled with stained furniture, mosquitoes, and dirty underwear?"

"I did not leave behind any underwear."

"That's what you have a problem with in that whole list, Dad? Underwear?"

"Chelsea, this woman is mental, and she is exaggerating. She's a loose lemon, and she is trying to get money from me. You can tell wealth on a man based on his stomach, and I, my dear, have a very wealthy stomach."

"This is the tenth letter we've had in the past three years asking for a refund. Do you even have any renters that *don't* ask for a refund?"

"What kind of question is that, Chelsea? I've been renting in the Vineyard for years, and anyone with any experience abroad knows that that piece of property is worth millions for the view alone."

"Dad, it's great that there's a nice view, but eventually people need to go inside and take a fucking shower."

"Chelsea..."

"You have more to think about than yourself now, because I do not want my name in the paper with a story about you being a crook. You need to refund her the money."

"Well, what are they going to write, exactly?"

"I don't know, and I don't want to know. I want you to refund the money ASAP. You need to FedEx it tomorrow, so she gets it Thursday at the latest."

"All right, all right, already." He took a bite out of something, which sounded like a dog trying to chew a bone. "Chelsea, this celebrity thing isn't easy on me either, you know. A lot of people are going to try and use it against us."

My head jutted forward like a giraffe that was about to neck-wrestle another giraffe. "Come again?"

"A lot of people stop me at the grocery store. They want to know about me, where I grew up, how I created such a successful comedian. They want to take me to dinner. Women, especially. Very flirtatious. Women see something in me, Chelsea."

I moved the phone away from my ear and snapped my fingers to get Ted's attention. My eyes were still rolling when it was my turn to interrupt.

"I'm sure that your celebrity status has been a real impediment to your lifestyle. Maybe if you stop opening your conversations with the fact that you're my father, people would stop harassing you about it. Or maybe you could just stop going to the grocery store five times a day. Maybe you should just stay indoors, like an inmate."

"Chelsea, that is not how you talk to your daddy."

"I told you to stop referring to yourself as Daddy, to me or anyone else for that matter. When will you be able to get to FedEx to mail the payment?"

"I'll get it out tomorrow. I'm not sending the whole refund. I'll send her two thousand dollars. She didn't ask for the whole refund."

"Send her five thousand dollars, and I would really appreciate you thinking twice before screwing anyone else over. I don't want you renting the house in that condition. Someone is going to sue you for a lot more than five thousand dollars, and you're going to be sorry. I'm sure the *Martha's Vineyard Times* is going to be keeping an eye on the situation, because the reporter said this isn't the first time he's heard your name mentioned in conjunction with unhappy renters."

"Really?" he asked, alarmed. "Well, the house is already rented for the next two weeks, so there's nothing I can do about that."

"Give me the cleaning lady's number from the Vineyard, and I'll make sure she gets everything taken care of before anyone else has to live in that filth."

"Cleaning lady is no good. She's not speaking to me right now. She insists on getting paid before the work gets done, and that's not how I operate."

"You don't know how to operate, that's the problem. She wants to get paid beforehand because you owe her and every other service person on that island money. You *need* an operation."

"I do not need an operation. I have a clean bill of health. Those Angus burgers at McDonald's are something else. Doctor said I'm in tip-top shape."

181

My father had had a quintuple bypass seven years prior and took that to mean that all his pipes were brand new and he had the ability to start fresh, like an infant. There was no way he was in good health, and there was certainly no way he had seen his doctor other than to get that prescription for Cialis.

"Call me after you send the money to Mrs. Danziger. She wants five thousand dollars. Are you clear?"

"Yeah, I'll send the money, but make sure she knows she is not welcome back."

"Okay, I'm hanging up now."

"Chelsea, hold the wire. So you haven't heard anything from the *Boston Globe*? I'm surprised this isn't something they'd be interested in picking up. *Martha's Vineyard Times* is pretty small potatoes."

I stared at the plane outside that was taking off from LAX, wondering why it couldn't just fly right into the living room my father was sitting in. "No, nothing from the *Boston Globe*. I'll call tomorrow to make sure you sent the check. No fucking around."

"Chelsea, there's no reason to use that kind of language."

Ted had taken off his reading glasses and was staring at me when I hung up the phone. "Please don't tell me he said what I think I just heard."

I sent an e-mail to my brothers and sisters informing them of the phone call and asking them to confirm the execution of the FedExing of the reimbursement. My

brother Greg responded to all of us with the suggestion of
our having our father euthanized, but after the New Year
so that the inheritance tax we'd owe for the properties he
owned wouldn't put us all in debt.

"I don't know any euthanizers personally, and I'm not
sure if that's a service that is publicly advertised, but I'll
ask around," I replied.

The next e-mail we received was from my oldest sister,
Sidney. "As an attorney, I am advising you all to cease and
desist any and all discussion of the euthanization of our
father via e-mail. I am available by phone at your earliest
convenience."

Chapter Nine

The Suspect

A week after my father reimbursed only one of the hundreds of dissatisfied renters he's had, my brother Greg sat him down for a grave intervention. Once Melvin realized that we were all serious about not providing him with any more financial dispensation, he became amenable to selling his main residence in Livingston, New Jersey. Greg took it upon himself to spearhead this debacle, mostly I believe because he has three small children and was looking to get out of his house. After his visit he sent a detailed account of the day to my brothers, sisters, and me.

September 17, 2008

4:30–6:45 P.M.

35 Morningside Drive

Dad—the suspect—is sitting out front on the porch basking in the warmth of a sunny and beautiful September afternoon.

Mariana Wallingford, a 46-year-old woman who hails from Livingston and claims she smoked pot in high school with Ray, saunters up Dad's decrepit driveway with her sidekick Realtor husband.

These two had also stopped by several days earlier to tour and assess the house and its ethereal state of utter disrepair. I left work early that day and ordered Dad off the premises in the hopes of giving our new Realtors as little contact with the suspect as possible. The showcase items Dad left behind in order to ensure a lofty appraisal were as follows: Three cabinet doors missing along with a can of soup on the kitchen island from the year 1995. A shutter on the second floor window missing and another shutter on the first floor in front of the living room resting gently on the bushes underneath it. The back room with the fireplace, which Platypus refers to as the "Blue Room" (despite there being no blue in the room), was covered in black mold. The upstairs linen closet had a hornet's nest, which was mildly surprising considering the landscaping bees are drawn to, and being that there are no living plants at 35 Morningside Drive.

I prepared both Realtors for their impending sit-down with Dad, and made them fully aware that they would be dealing with a very delusional, irrational, but nonviolent, common-day lunatic. I assured them I would be there to supervise the meeting and hopefully prevent Dad from demolishing a hot pastrami on rye in their presence.

On the day of the meeting, Dad answers the front door in a pair of sweatpants and a sweater Mom knit for him from the earlier part of the previous century. The four of us move inside and up in the living room, where everyone sits down so they can make their gay and pointless real estate presentation.

We get down to the only relevant point and they indi-cate that the most favorable listing price to create potential multiple bids is $699,000. This is the same number Ray's Realtor came up with one or two months ago and shared with the suspect. (Dad leisurely answers two calls on his cell phone during the middle of the meeting. He takes his time on the phone while everyone else waits around like a jackass.) I indicate to the suspect that I agree with the Realtors and fully and articulately explain to the suspect that the listing price is only the "listing price" and you generally wind up receiving bids above that number; I am careful to re-explain that the listing price is not the "selling price"— it's merely a widely practiced marketing ploy to produce a higher selling price; this well-accepted practice was then illustrated with actual sales examples of many nearby properties that actually sold for well above their listing prices.

Dad indicates his disagreement with the $699,000 number and proceeds to compare his property to other properties that are actually inhabitable and that sold for much more money. He mentions how he cleaned the mold in the "Blue Room" with some soap and it comes right off, so that problem is solved; I mentioned that remediating the mold scenario was actually a minimum $10,000–$20,000 reconstruction job (i.e., the insides of the walls are all consumed with industrial strength mold—some wall sections are bleached black from mold consumption). We all discuss the idea of selling the house "as is" since selling it not "as is" would require $200,000 to make the entire structure habitable. He agrees. He wants to list it at $749,000 or $739,000, and we get him down to $729,000.

Midway through this episode, we are pleasantly and appropriately interrupted by a knock at the open front door by a service person from the cable company. He shouts from the front door that he needs to pick up payment on the past-due cable bill. Dad says to me, "Greg, you want to give him a check." I say, "He's your vendor." Dad says, "I'll pay you next week," from the upper living room to the service guy still standing outside the front door whom no one can actually see. The cable guy says, "Then I have to pick up your cable box now." Dad says, "Go ahead and take it." The cable guy says, "I'm not allowed to go in the house and take it myself; you have to give it to me." I say to the invisible cable guy, "We're in the middle of a meeting selling the house. Can you come back another time?" The cable guy says, "Okay, but you'll have to bring the cable equipment to our office within one week." Dad says, "Okay…" The never-seen cable guy departs, not knowing or caring that Dad would sooner participate in an octogenarian potato-sack race before setting foot inside any cable office to return anything.

Platypus then proceeds to question Mariana's enthusiasm for the sale. For the record, Mariana and her hubby typically sell about 50 properties a year. I had just met her for the first time, and she seemed like a very nice, honest, straightforward, mild-mannered, but effective, salesperson. Dad says, "You mentioned you've been in the industry for 20 years…well, Mariana, I think you've lost some of your enthusiasm over the years. You haven't said one positive thing about this house since you saw it the other day.…I don't think you like this house.…"

The life leaks out of everyone's bodies. It's clear that Mariana has never heard anything approaching this type of indictment in her entire career. Mariana says she's sorry if she gave that impression and that she likes the house fine. Platypus continues to question her enthusiasm, her spirit and her lack of regard for his decrepit castle. Mariana's husband then tells us how he bought his own home from Mariana a few years back and that is how they came to work together and fall deeply into one another's arms. Mariana's husband says what a great person and salesperson Mariana has been over the years, and that after both of their divorces, they felt so lucky to not only have found each other but were also fortunate enough to start a realty company. Later on in the meeting, Mariana mentions that her only daughter, whose 17th birthday is today, has been a mute since she witnessed her cousin being attacked and killed by a shark in Hawaii five years ago. Nice going, Platypus.

After Dad has one of his disgusting coughing attacks, somehow the sales process resumes and the suspect signs the Real Estate Listing agreement. I fill out the seller's property disclosure statement on the suspect's behalf, thereby indicating on paper that the seller is *not aware* that the property is uninhabitable in every regard. Platypus proceeds to regale Mariana and her husband with tales of the house, Mom, Martha's Vineyard, the symbolic and big bloody bull painting above his head, as they both look at the painting, horrified. At this precise moment, a loud crash is heard from the kitchen area. Mariana, her husband, and I all jump at what sounds like an AK-47 gunshot as Platypus turns his head slightly with no reaction whatsoever. The four of us get up from the living room and walk down the five steps into the kitchen, where we discover an eagle with a wingspan of at least five feet sprawled outside the now shattered sliding glass door.

In complete alarm, I gently slide open the glass door to take a closer look at the bird in order to determine if he has indeed taken his own life. In a shocking twist, the eagle's wings began to flutter slowly, and somehow, unbelievably, the bird gets his wits about him and is able to fly away. Dad dismisses the incident with a wave of his hand, the same way he would react to finding out there was going to be a rain delay for today's Mets game.

Mariana regains a modicum of composure as her husband is hugging her and she shakily proceeds to tell the suspect how the sales process is anticipated to proceed; the suspect indicates he'd "like a courtesy call" before any visitors show up. The session winds down and is adjourned thanks to Allah, Jesus, and Satan.

I walked the appalled couple out to their car and thanked them for their time.

I then went back inside 35 Morningside, where Dad had already made his way to the kitchen for some heavy carb-loading and a diet peach Snapple. The suspect mentioned how his fax was not working, and I went to go check on it. He casually mentioned something about the phone company restricting it, which of course meant he hadn't paid his phone bill and they'd disconnected the phone service. I mentioned that paying his phone bill would fix his fax.

I then issued the suspect a loan check for $9,900, repayable to me through the sales proceeds of his castle, kissed the suspect on the upper left side of his face and departed.

If Platypus refuses to shape up, I again would like to suggest the option of Euthanization. Or we can put him down like a horse.

Upon receipt of this e-mail, my sister Sidney was the first to respond:

From: **Sidney Handler**
September 17th, 2008 10:20 AM

Sounds like a great afternoon. Good work. On a more pathetic note, I just got a call from Dad—only he has this kind of luck. Apparently a small mouse got into the house on the Vineyard and climbed under the fridge—got into the motor and, well, that led to the mouse's untimely and gory demise. The kitchen stinks to high heaven and the renters are looking for an alternative place to live. After striking out with the usual Vineyard suspects, Dad's next bright idea was to have Jeff [Sidney's husband] drive up there today and take a look at the fridge. Apparently Dad is unaware that Jeff is gainfully employed and doesn't work at the Dairy Queen....I advised Dad that Jeff wasn't available and his refrigerator repairman's license has never existed. I told him to contact the local fridge supplier pronto and get a replacement and worry about the details and cost later....This will most likely end with Dad being hung up on, since no one on the island will do business with him. Euthanasia is illegal, and therefore not an option.

I'm thinking about changing my last name to Lately.

Sent via BlackBerry

FROM: **SLOANE HANDLER**
SENT: **SEPT** 18 11:58:54 2008
SUBJECT: PLATYPUS RULES

SORRY, I'VE BEEN BUSY WITH ONLINE PHOTO SHARING, FORGOT TO TELL YOU ABOUT THE LATEST INSTALLMENT OF UNHAPPY RENTING. DAD BELIEVES THE MOUSE WAS A RESULT OF AROMATIC CURRIES BEING COOKED BY THE RENTERS WHO WERE "UNUSUALLY BLACK" AND, THEREFORE, ATTRACTED TO SPICE.

PLATYPUS JUST LEFT HERE....HE'S GOT BIG PLANS TO SUE THE HAITIAN RENTERS FOR COOKING FATTY GREASY FOODS THAT SMELLED

UP THE HOUSE AND ATTRACTED A RODENT, THEREBY CAUSING THE FOLLOWING WEEK'S RENTERS TO BAIL ONCE THEY GOT A WHIFF.... SO HE LOST THAT WEEK'S INCOME, CLAIMS THEY ALSO RUINED THE DECK WITH "BURN MARKS AND VINEGAR STAINS....PROBABLY RELATED TO VOODOO AND WITCHCRAFT, ACTING LIKE CANNIBALS...AND USING POOR HYGIENE!!!" SOUNDS LIKE A SUREFIRE WINNER!

FROM: **RAY HANDLER**
SENT: SEPT 19 10:01:54 2008
SUBJECT: THE HITS JUST KEEP ON COMING
   I NORMALLY SLEEP FROM MIDNIGHT TO 4 AM. LAST NIGHT, I TRIED SOMETHING DIFFERENT.
   12:05 AM RECEIVE PHONE CALL **FROM** SLOTIME (SLOANE), WHO INDICATES THAT I NEED TO CALL DAD ASAP.
   12:10 CALL PLATYPUS; HE INDICATES HE NEEDS AN ALLENTOWN, PENNSYLVANIA, PICK-UP; SINCE I'M THE ONLY ONE WITHOUT A FAMILY OR A GIRLFRIEND, HE INDICATES THAT IT MAKES THE MOST SENSE FOR ME TO PICK HIM UP.
   12:15 DEPART WEST CALDWELL, NJ.
   1:30 ARRIVE AT SUNOCO STATION, WHERE MOM'S VAN HAS BEEN TOWED TO IN ALLENTOWN, PA; THE VEHICLE HAD OVERHEATED AND THE ENGINE WAS SHOT.

1:35 PAY $123 FOR HIS TOW CHARGE BECAUSE HE HAS NO CASH AND DOESN'T UNDERSTAND WHY HIS SUNOCO GAS CARD DOESN'T ALSO ALLOW HIM TO WITHDRAW CASH.

1:40 DEPART ALLENTOWN WITH MELVIN **AND** HIS 22-YEAR-OLD BLACK MAID **AND** HER SIMILARLY AGED AND PIGMENTED GIRLFRIEND.

1:45 SMALL TALK FROM DAD ABOUT HOW HE HAD TAKEN THE TWO GIRLS TO NEARBY DORNEY PARK (ROLLER COASTERS, WATER SLIDES AND OTHER FUN THINGS FOR 75-YEAR-OLD MEN) FOR THE DAY BECAUSE HE HAD PROMISED TO DRIVE THEM THERE.

2:00 AFTER MELVIN WONDERS ALOUD WHY YOU NEED A SEPARATE ATM CARD AND WHAT EXACTLY A PIN IS, I TELL HIM WHY A PIN IS REQUIRED FOR AN ATM CARD, AND THAT SUNOCO GAS CARDS ARE CREDIT CARDS FOR THE SUNOCO GAS STATION ONLY, NOT CASH CARDS. THIS IS NEW AND SHOCK-ING INFORMATION FOR MELVIN.

2:10 MELVIN COMMENTS ON THE "SMOOTH RIDE" OF THE MERCEDES E320.

2:50 MELVIN GIVES ME DRIVING INSTRUCTIONS TO THE GIRLS' EAST ORANGE NEIGHBORHOOD THAT ARE COMPLETELY OUT OF THE WAY, INEFFICIENT AND DANGEROUS, SINCE THEY GO THROUGH SOME OF THE WORST INNER-GHETTO SIDE STREETS OF NEWARK. THE GIRLS START SNAPPING AT HIM THAT HE'S GOING COMPLETELY OUT OF THE WAY AND THE

WRONG WAY. MELVIN TELLS ONE OF THE GIRLS TO
"SAVE IT."

3:05 PROCEED THROUGH SOME OF THE SCARIEST
STREETS I HAVE EVER SEEN IN MY LIFE. OCCASIONAL
DERELICTS WALK AIMLESSLY AND MENACINGLY
THROUGH THE STREETS. I WONDER HOW I'M GOING
TO ARTICULATE MY LIKELY IMMINENT BODILY INJURIES/
STOLEN CAR/AND OR DEATH TO THE FAMILY AND
GIRLFRIEND I DON'T HAVE.

3:10 SOMEHOW, WE MAKE IT TO THEIR EAST
ORANGE NEIGHBORHOOD AND THE GIRLS ARE
INCREASINGLY HURLING BITTER AND ANGRY
INSULTS AT DAD FOR SOME REAL OR IMAGINED
TRANSGRESSIONS. THEY GO FOR THE FULL
MELTDOWN AND DEMAND TO GET OUT OF THE
CAR IMMEDIATELY. I STOP, THEY EXIT THE VEHICLE IN
A HUFF, AND WE PROCEED AWAY AS A DARKENED
POLICE CAR LURKS DOWN THE BLOCK.

3:11 THE EAST ORANGE POLICE AND A BACK-UP
PULL US OVER AND ASK ME FOR MY PAPERWORK. THEN
THEY ASK US WHAT THE HELL WAS GOING ON. I SAY I
WAS PERFORMING LIVERY SERVICES FOR POPSICLE AND
HIS MAID/FRIEND. HE ASKS ME TO STEP TO THE REAR
OF THE VEHICLE AND THEN TELLS ME PRIVATELY THAT
THE TWO INDIVIDUALS WE JUST DROPPED OFF ARE
WELL-KNOWN LADIES OF THE NIGHT AND OUR BEHAV-
IOR LOOKS PRETTY SUSPICIOUS, TO PUT IT MILDLY. HE
ADVISES ME TO STAY OUT OF EAST ORANGE.

3:30 POPSICLE MENTIONS THAT WHEN YOU HANG AROUND WITH GARBAGE PEOPLE, THE END RESULT WILL BE GARBAGE.

3:40 DROP POPSICLE AT 35 MORNINGSIDE DRIVE. HE POINTS TO ONE OF THE DECREPIT JALOPIES IN HIS DRIVEWAY AND PROUDLY PROCLAIMS, "THERE'S MY NEW VEHICLE."

4:00 AM ARRIVE IN WEST CALDWELL.

9:04 AM SHOW UP BRIGHT-EYED AND BUSHY-TAILED TO MY JOB. HOW MUCH IS EUTHANASIA? AND WHAT IS EUTHANASIA?

FROM: **CHELSEA HANDLER**
RE: THE HITS JUST KEEP ON COMING
TIME: SEPT 19, 11:10:43
PLEASE TELL ME THIS DID NOT REALLY HAPPEN. IF THIS IS A TRUE STORY, I THINK WE SHOULD HAVE HIM COMMITTED. SIDNEY?

From: **Sidney Handler**
Re: The Hits Just Keep on Coming
Time: Sept 18, 2008 12:10:34
We can't commit him to an institution because he knows the date, time, and the president of the United States. I have looked into this, and even though he's completely out of step with modern-day society, he still has all his faculties. Poor Mom, she's probably rolling over in her grave that he didn't even pay for.
Sent via BlackBerry

FROM: **SLOANE HANDLER**
TIME: SEPT 18, 12:38:34
SUBJECT: THE HITS JUST KEEP ON COMING
   OBJECTION!!! HE DOES NOT HAVE ALL HIS
FACULTIES. HE DEFINITELY PEED ON MY SOFA
THE OTHER DAY. I HAVE TO PUT NEWSPAPER
DOWN WHEN HE COMES OVER! ISN'T THAT ALL
THE PROOF WE NEED? HE THINKS HE'S COM-
ING WITH US TO PUERTO RICO FOR CHRISTMAS,
BUT I THINK WE SHOULD TELL HIM CHRISTMAS
IS ON A DIFFERENT DAY THIS YEAR, BECAUSE
HE WILL ONLY EMBARRASS US, AND I'M WOR-
RIED ABOUT CHELSEA'S AND MY PROFILE. HER
CAREER HAS HAD AN ASTONISHINGLY POSITIVE
EFFECT ON MY SOCIAL LIFE, AND I'VE BEEN
CONTACTED VIA FACEBOOK BY ALMOST EVERY
PERSON IN HIGH SCHOOL THAT WAS MEAN TO
ME. I'M NOT PREPARED TO TAKE TWO STEPS
BACK AT THIS JUNCTURE. AND WHY DOES HE
NEED A HOOKER IF HE HAS A GIRFLRIEND?

FROM: **CHELSEA HANDLER**
TIME: SEPT 18 12:45:55
SUBJECT: THE HITS JUST KEEP ON COMING
   SLOANE, ARE YOU STUPID? OBVIOUSLY, HIS
GIRLFRIEND *IS* A HOOKER.
   MOM IS NOT ROLLING OVER IN HER GRAVE,
SHE IS LAUGHING HER ASS OFF. SHE WARNED

US ALL THAT HE IS A BIG ASSHOLE, AND THAT
ONCE SHE WAS GONE, THERE WOULD BE NO
ONE TO KEEP HIS BEHAVIOR IN CHECK. I'M NOT
ENTIRELY SURE THAT EUTHANIZATION IS STILL
ILLEGAL. WHAT DOES THAT REQUIRE?

From: **Greg Handler**
Time: Sept 18 12:59:01 P.M.
Subject: The Hits Just Keep on Coming

Chelsea, Google Dr. Jack Kevorkian, and you can educate yourself on euthanizing someone. I believe Mario, Dad's new mozzarella-stick friend, has some low-level Mafia ties. With *The Sopranos* off the air, there's also plenty of the cast members who are no longer employed, and I'm sure one or more would be open to making a cool three hundred and fifty dollars. A different approach, but effective nonetheless.

Girls, cool it with the all caps. Ray invented capitalizing all words and proper misspelling.

FROM: **CHELSEA HANDLER**
TIME: SEPT 18 1:05:18 P.M.
SUBJECT: THE HITS JUST KEEP ON COMING

ANOTHER OPTION WOULD BE FOR EACH OF
US TO KILL OURSELVES. WHO'S WITH ME?

From: **SIDNEY HANDLER**
Time: SEPT 18 1:25:19 P.M.
Subject: PLATYPUS RULES

If you killed yourself, Ted would kill himself, and we shouldn't be involving any other families. Let's please try and keep the hooker tale between each other and not tell spouses and/or boyfriends. This isn't something I want people knowing about.

As an attorney, I am advising all of you to stop sending emails regarding "a hit" and/or euthanasia at this time. Please call me immediately.

Sent via BlackBerry

The next week my father got a bid on his house to the tune of $600,000 and then threatened to sue the Asian family for making such a low offer. Shortly after, my brother showed him his latest legal bill, which was in the amount of $23,000 and was from a law firm that he tried to sue for malpractice after they lost my father's case to make our neighbors cut down *their* trees in *their* own yard. His issue: They were pine trees and, being a Jew, my father does not appreciate Christmas trees being shoved in his face. He believed they were anti-Semitic trees and that the people living behind those trees were clearly Nazi sympathizers. Shortly after that, Greg showed him Exhibit B: a judgment from the Martha's Vineyard court against my father in the amount of $17,000, for a case he lost when he tried to represent himself pro se against our other neighbors, who no longer wanted to share their path to the beach with my father, because he usually walks down naked.

After a little negotiating with the nice Asian family, they were finally able to come up to $625,000. This proved to be perfect timing for the last thing Greg was holding in

his arsenal. It was Platypus's bank statement, which said
−$42.67.

This was the day my father sold his home, and after all the
bills and payments he needed to pay to clear his name (that
we know about), he was left with a little over $400,000.

He agreed for Greg to be a cosigner on his account,
which gave Greg access to monitor our father's account, as
well as the right to deny Platypus money if the amount of
any charge exceeds $1,000. Like a child. A very bad child
who urinates on other people's furniture.

By February my brother had sent us a litany of charges
on my father's latest monthly debit-card breakdown, which
showed a total of $201,000. Most were large but not inor-
dinate amounts at the local McDonald's, which he seemed
to frequent three times a day. Others were payments to
nightclubs in Newark, and one big charge was a Delta Air
Lines flight for $754, which was dubious since my father
doesn't fly. There were four separate charges for Sean John
tracksuits, and a few basketball jerseys, plus a Bluetooth.

I called Greg and asked him how it was possible to
blow $200,000 in five months.

"Well, Chelsea, he's either buying a hundred Angus
burgers a day or flying to different parts of the country to
visit other McDonald's."

"What?"

"That's right. There's two of them. He and his twenty-
year-old cleaning hooker are seeing the Grand Ol' U.S. of
A.! They're on their way to the Grand Canyon right now."

"Please tell me you're kidding."

"No, Chelsea. He's in great spirits and mailed me a poem he sent Mom thirty years ago that he wants you to put in your new book. He said he has a feeling he isn't going to be shown in the best light, because 'Chelsea has a tendency to confuse the details,' and he doesn't want to disappoint his fans. He wants to offer you the poem for a cool $25,000."

"What did you tell him?"

"I told him that I'm thinking of a phrase that begins with an 'F' and ends with an 'F.' Would he like to buy a vowel?"

"And?"

"He did not want to purchase a vowel."

★ ★ ★

SONNET TO SYLVIA III

(The poem my father wanted $25,000 dollars for, but never got.)

> I would send roses, stars to my beloved,
> bouquets sweet
> and bar no lilies from her feet.
> Oh, I would send thrushes and martins skyward.
> Hers alone would I be: how sure of love
> we, who see only one another;
> such blindness like a wind-swept sea, becalmed
> becomes a kindness soon.
> The ships sail homeward seeking port.
> Love, unskilled but true, moves onward,
> lost in the wake of arms and kisses,
> then awakening at last, sees itself.
> Storms and seas and kisses run aground
> only love that's lost is ever found.

Chapter Ten

Chunk

Flying Southwest Airlines is analogous to being the last one picked for kickball in the third grade. Initially, an "A" boarding pass feels like you've bypassed some system flaw and managed to come out one step ahead of the game. Getting your preference of any row and then, on top of that, having your choice of window, aisle, or middle seat feels borderline aristocratic. When that "A" boarding pass comes flying out of the ticket kiosk into your palm, the whole airport experience shifts from Dora the Explorer to Princess Grace of Monaco.

That sensation quickly turns around once several "B" passengers walk by and look at you like they'd rather catch herpes from back-to-back elephant sex than share a row with you. The excitement of picking the middle seat in the hopes that none of the passengers will bother to sit right next to you soon diminishes into fear and shame that no one even *wants* to sit next to you. Traveler after traveler rejects you, causing any spike in self-esteem from nabbing an "A" ticket to plummet into LaToya Jackson territory.

"Fuck off," I wanted to tell the leathery, turban-headed anorexic who saw a more appealing seatmate farther down the plane. "Fuck you and the camel you rode in on." I generally don't start farting until the plane's in the air, so the rejection definitely was not ass-related. I was being tossed aside like a piece of Styrofoam before anyone had even bothered to inquire about my hobbies and/or predilection for prescription pills.

I vowed never to fly Southwest again, but Sarah was having her bachelorette weekend in San Francisco, and her maid of honor booked us all on the only airline that had managed to find pilots and a crew who also happened to be hilarious stand-up comedians.

Normally I would book my own flight for such affairs, but I didn't want to rock the boat for two reasons: (a) This was Sarah's second engagement, so I wanted things to go off without a hitch, and (b) I was physically frightened of her maid of honor, Tanya.

Tanya is a friend from Sarah's childhood, and even though I've met her several times over the years, she still seems somewhat shy until she polishes off three to seven

Guinness stouts and then forces you to arm-wrestle her. Although I take pride in working out on a semiregular basis, I do not consider myself capable of winning any sort of wrestling match with a boy, a girl, or any sort of Pacific Islander descendant. I get incredibly anxious when challenged to any test of strength and usually end up pulling a groin muscle no matter where the area of strength being challenged is centralized.

I had steered clear of Tanya for the better part of the weekend, but on the last night in San Francisco we all came back to the main suite to continue drinking, and Tanya slowly but surely transformed herself into Michael Vick. Two of the girls had passed out on the floor, and I knew that being trapped in a hotel room with a dwindling crowd was going to minimize my ability to outmaneuver her.

I was doing everything in my wheelhouse to avoid a one on one altercation. I averted eye contact when she tackled an innocent lamp that had said and done nothing to her. When I saw an eight-hour-old chicken finger fly through the living room into the bedroom and heard it split in two, I looked yonder. When gummy bears were being hauled in the direction of my head, with one in particular landing inside my ear, I intercepted further missiles with my hand, deftly masking my movement by cupping my ear and pretending to hear knocking on the door. I did not want to give in to the bully and let her know I found her teasing considerably disappointing.

I did, however, step in when she called room service requesting an omelet with three black men inside. I grabbed the phone out of her hand and told the person on the other end of the phone, *"Black beans.* An omelet with *black beans*, please." I hung up the phone, unplugged it from the wall, and hid it in my suitcase.

"God, Chelsea," Sarah said, trying to light a cigarette with the remote control. "You've really turned into a killjoy."

"Did you really just hide the phone?" Tanya asked me as I stood with my hands on my hips. I knew by their reactions that certain measures were going to be dealt as a warning to me and my body.

One by one, the remaining six of us were forced to arm-wrestle again and again. It wasn't Tanya's strength that I found intimidating; it was the starry, retarded way her eyes focused on me, like Mike Tyson getting ready to feed. I didn't even try to put up a fight the first few times, but the celebratory high-fiving and hooting, combined with half a gummy bear's torso still stuck to my eardrum, were reason to grow delirious.

"Fine, you fucker, let's go!" I yelled, getting into position on the floor while my friend Shannon video-recorded what would inevitably turn into a violent episode of *The L Word.* I hoped I could turn my anger and humiliation into a sort of rabies strength but was reminded time and again who was in charge. Losing in conjunction with the stadium cheering wasn't the worst part; after she beat each one of us, she would leapfrog onto the back of our heads, crushing our faces into the carpeting, and then spank us. It was beyond embarrassing.

The next morning was pretty painful for everyone, and our ride to the airport was quiet. Once we boarded the plane, however, a surge of energy overtook the girls and the conversation quickly turned to Sarah's honeymoon on safari and whether she was planning on letting her fiancé fertilize her first egg in the African bush. All the rest of us went through our timelines for children, and inevitably, even though I had put on my eyeshades and was trying to avoid participating in any conversation, I was the last one left to harass.

"I don't want kids," I said without taking off my eye-shades. "That's why I take the morning-after pill every morning, whether I've had sex the night before or not. I also take calcium to keep my bones strong, and Ted and I take Ensure just to stay active." I didn't have the energy or interest in a real conversation and was secretly hoping that Tanya wouldn't order a Bloody Mary when the sky waitress approached. "Has anyone here tried Boniva?" I asked the group.

"You should *so* have a baby," Tanya advised me.

"Of course she should," Sarah agreed. "She acts like she hates kids, but it's not true. Just look at how she was last night, like a camp counselor. Hiding the phone from us.

You're going to change your mind, Chelsea. You'll probably end up with more kids than any of us. Just wait."

I would rather sit next to a transgender person and discuss why every single one I've met smells like a bar in the daytime than listen to people tell me why I want to have children and that I just don't know it yet. I do know, because I'm me and my feelings are the ones in my head. I don't want to have kids, and it's not a device to get attention or have conversations about it. I simply find children incredibly immature and, more often than not, dumb.

"Oh, my God!" Tanya wailed. "Look at this poor dog!" She handed me her BlackBerry so I could look at the picture of the canine. "He's redlined, so they're going to kill him on Monday in San Diego unless you rescue him." I pushed up my eyeshades to see who she was talking to and realized it was me. "He's so sweet. He's beautiful," she persisted.

"Then you get him," I said.

"I just rescued Lucifer three months ago, and he's really skittish still. I have four, and my husband says we're at our limit."

"What about Sarah?" I asked.

"I live in an apartment," Sarah replied, opening a magazine to signal that this wasn't a conversation she was interested in pursuing. Then, for good measure, she snickered and added, "Chelsea, you've been trying to rescue a dog for months."

I didn't have the energy to turn around and punch Sarah in the coslopus. I wanted Tanya to stop talking. I wanted to stop hearing about kids and dogs and even Beyoncé if she were to come up. I was weak from the wrestling and from the detox cleanse that Ivory, Sarah, Tanya, and I decided to start that morning. The three of us had committed to do it together in anticipation of Sarah's wedding and were excited at the prospect of losing ten to forty-seven pounds in six days. I had already ordered a thermal track suit to assist in shedding any additional bloat. Like every other time I've tried to deprive myself of food, my head was slowly spinning and a wave of nausea was throwing my equilibrium off course.

I looked at the picture, looked at the tarmac that hadn't started moving yet, and felt feverish. I wondered how long it would take me to get my hands on some Excedrin once the plane landed, and then I wondered how cavemen dealt with hangovers without access to Excedrin. I looked at Tanya, who was staring me down from the seat next to me, and thought that she would have made a good caveman. If getting a dog was what it was going to take to end the conversation so I could sleep, then that's what it was going to take. "Fine. I'll have Eva pick him up tomorrow."

"Who's Eva?" Tanya demanded.

"My assistant."

"You can't have your assistant pick him up, Chelsea. You need to bond with him," she advised me, gripping my wrist very aggressively. I pulled my hand away with a buoyed confidence; we were in public, and she was less likely to harm me with so many witnesses. I was fed up with Tanya and wanted her off my jock.

"I hate to break it to you, but I have a job that requires me to actually be there during the day. I once saw a special on rescuing dogs, and the interview process is more complicated than the one for buying a cleft-palated Vietnamese adolescent. I don't really have time to head to the L.A. pound for a cool four and a half hours during my lunch break. I said I'd get the dog, okay? Can we just press on to something else, like when you're going to confront the fact that you're most likely a lesbian who wants to work as a night guard at a women's detention center?"

Sarah shot me a look, and I changed my tune quickly.

The last occasion when I'd spent time with Sarah's friends from childhood was when her previous wedding was called off and we all gathered at Tanya's mom's house in Brentwood for moral support. For reasons still unknown to me, I took the breakup harder than anyone else, including Sarah. After three days of me sleeping over at Sarah's apartment with the two of us in her bed and me waking up each morning in tears, Sarah basically told me she needed a break.

"I think we need some time apart," she informed me while I was folding her laundry one afternoon and watching *Another World*. "I've been dumped, I have a wedding to cancel, and I need you to accept it and move on. You need to get your life going in the right direction. It's not healthy for me to be sitting around here every day watching daytime television while you're in a housedress."

I *was* bringing her down. I had felt so blindsided by the breakup that I didn't know if I would ever be able to date again.

After that it took a while for any of her friends to accept the fact that I wasn't deranged, and I didn't want to cause any more rumblings now. I wanted them to know that I was normal and healthy and could take on responsibilities without shitting my pants.

"I'll get the dog myself," I told Tanya. "I promise."

I did intend to get the dog, but I had zero intention of actually picking it up from the pound. Largely because the words "Los Angeles" came before the word "pound," and the words "Los Angeles" at the beginning of any establishment's name imply to me large, smelly, disorganized rooms filled with large, smelly, disorganized people. My last experience with a circus tent of that caliber was with the L.A. County Women's Prison. L.A. Free Clinic, L.A. Animal Shelter, LAPD—you name it, they all sound appalling. "Los Angeles" came to have the same negative connotation as the word "adult" before something: adult braces, adult diapers, adult acne—all incredibly discouraging.

The day after we returned from the bachelorette weekend, I woke up hallucinating in a pool of my own detoxification sweat. Twenty-four hours of not eating any real food and chugging three thirty-eight-ounce concoctions of something brown had taken their toll on my pituitary gland. By 8:00 A.M. I had vomited three times and made the executive decision that my body had too many toxins to release. Ted looked at me with my head inside the toilet and gently reminded me that starting a cleanse after a weekend of drinking wasn't the smartest life choice for me or my vessel.

"I was trying to do it in solidarity with Sarah for the wedding," I whimpered, with one hand on the side of the cold toilet and the other hand making a chignon out of the hair I was trying to keep from falling in.

"Cleanses are stupid, honey," he said, shaking his head. "Can I get you some ginger ale, or water, or oatmeal?"

"Yes, Ted. Oatmeal sounds fabulous right now. Do we have enough for three bowls?"

Instead I stopped by Del Taco on my way in to work. I ordered a breakfast burrito, and when the drive-through attendant asked if I wanted hash browns or french fries, I yelled, "BOTH, BITCH!" Then I took a picture of the drive-through window on my camera phone and e-mailed it to Ivory and Sarah with a heading attached that read "Breakfast." I didn't e-mail Tanya for obvious reasons.

Eva confirmed that she received my e-mail about the dog but wanted to verify that I was serious about getting it before she headed to the pound. "What if he's a bad dog or something's really wrong with him when I get there?" she asked me. "Do you want me to just make a judgment call, or should I bring him back no matter what?"

"Yeah, I guess. I don't know. Whatever you think."

"Okay, got it," she told me. "Let me just finish alphabetizing your makeup, and I'll try and get back to the office before lunch. And what about Ted? Does he know about this?"

"Yes," I lied.

Eva and Ted were in cahoots, and if you wanted to keep something from one of them, it was best to lie to both.

I was sitting in my partner Tom's office getting ready to tape the show when Eva walked in with the dog. "Here he is!" she said, panting. "They said at the pound that they think he's half chow, half German shepherd, and he's a really good dog. He knows how to sit and give a paw, and his paperwork says his name is Guinness, but his tag says Princess Leia."

"Is he a cross-dresser?" I asked her.

She frowned. "I don't know, but he really *is* good. I kind of can't believe it." Normally Eva can't be trusted for a real opinion, because she refuses to say anything negative—not my favorite quality in a person—but from what I could deduce, she seemed to be right about the dog.

He was wagging his tail and gently sniffing my coslopus. I stood up in order for the dog to get ahold of himself and assessed the situation. He looked like the dog I grew up with, Whitefoot.

"Are you Whitefoot?" I asked the dog, and waited patiently for a response. "Whitefoot? Is that you?" He wasn't responding to that name, and after I got out my pocket calculator and tapped some buttons, I gave up hope when I realized that Whitefoot would be 247 years old had he faked his own death.

"Chunk" is the nickname I give to anyone I love who I also want to squeeze. I called my mom "Chunk," and she called me "Chunky" when we would snuggle in bed together and I would squeeze her one boob. She had a mastectomy when I was nine and never bothered to get reconstructive surgery, so on one side she had a rice pack that she put in her bra every morning, and on the other side was a giant booby. I call Chuy "Chunk," and I call Ted "Chunk," and of course Sylvan is my "Chocolate Chunk."

My mother, Chunk

"His name will be Chunk," I announced, and then we kissed. After that he followed me everywhere I went. I had to go downstairs to do the show, and when I came back up thirty minutes later, he was standing in the same exact position right outside the elevator. When I went into the bathroom, he followed me in there, and when I closed the stall door for some adult privacy, he slid his body underneath the door and sat directly in front of me while I peed. We had a connection, and, most important, Chunk didn't talk or bark. When he did open his mouth to say something, I said in a very authoritative voice, "NO TALKING!" and he shut it again. After work that day, he hopped right into my car, and he sat in the backseat with his nose on my console. I lowered the windows so he could feel the moist marina wind blow through his snout. "You will eventually need goggles," I informed him.

We got home that night, and I took him for a walk while I braced myself to clean up a giant doggy shadoobie. My childhood experiences involving dog feces had never begun or ended well, and I knew that this was what had held me back from getting a dog earlier in my adult life. Vomit and feces are two reasons I have decided not to procreate. That and the fact that I never want to see the inside of Disney World or a Chuck E. Cheese again. Even as a toddler, I found both establishments insulting. I grabbed the plastic bag available outside the dog run and knew I was at a crossroads, not unlike Beyoncé in *Dreamgirls*. I was turning a corner, and that corner involved a dog's bowel movement.

Right away Chunk and I understood each other. He couldn't do it. He squatted to drop his deuce, then looked at me, then stood back up and ran over to me. I even let him off his leash to allow extra relaxation, but as long as he could smell me, he refused to shadoobie.

The most amazing part was that he was free to escape me permanently but would keep running back to me. I had never had a dog in my life that didn't try to escape when presented with the opportunity, although, in complete fairness, I would have left our family, too, had I had the financial capabilities. Anytime Mutley or Whitefoot, the dogs from my childhood, got loose, we'd have to get into the car and drive around the neighborhood, leaning on the horn, trying to trick the dog into coming back. "Come on, Whitefoot, let's go for a ride," my dad would yell through a megaphone he stole from my softball practice. "Get in the goddamned car!"

When Ted arrived home that night, I said, "Chunk, this is Chunk." Then I turned to Ted and said, "Chunk, meet Chunk."

"What is that?" Ted asked.

"It's a cat."

"*Whose* is it?"

"He's ours now."

"Very funny. Whose dog is it?"

"He is *our* dog. I captured him. They were going to assassinate him, Ted. He was going to be put in the electric chair. He's a rescue, like Chuy."

"Chelsea, can you cut the shit, please? We've already had one dog escapade this year. I'm not really in the mood to deal with Dudley Part Deux. You don't even like dogs."

"There is no shit to cut. This was a moment of weakness born out of a moment of detoxification. I like this dog. He seems to understand me and the pickle I've found myself in."

"What pickle is that?"

I eyed Ted and cocked my head to the side. "Wanting someone to snuggle with who doesn't speak."

"Did it ever occur to you to maybe ask me if I wanted to weigh in on the decision, since I live here, too?"

"Not really."

"Chelsea, a dog is a big decision, and we both travel all the time. Who do you think is going to take care of it?"

"Ray is moving here in three days. He loves dogs. It will be his welcoming gift, just like my father's frozen calamari for the renters on the Vineyard. My brother loves dogs."

Ted darted his eyes back and forth between the dog and me, not knowing what to believe. "I'm not stupid. You obviously borrowed the dog from someone."

"Who would I borrow a dog from? You don't borrow dogs from people. You either steal them or find them. Since when are there loaner dogs available?"

"Chelsea, please stop. I've had a long day, and I'm really just not in the mood. This is like that mini-horse you said you were buying for your sister." The mini-horse he was referencing was not a joke at all, and if it was, the joke ended up being on me.

Chuy and I had to take our annual Christmas photo, and one of my producers suggested bringing in a mini-horse he knew about that maybe Chuy could ride. The horse was about three feet tall, and upon sight I made an offer to his trainer, Bruce, to purchase him. Bruce was a giant dick and feigned surprise bordering on disgust when I asked him how much he wanted for the horse.

"This little fella's not for sale," he informed me. "They take a lot of work, a lot of attention," he said with a snicker. Then he added, "And they don't like *vodka*."

I wanted to kick Bruce in the taint. No one is just one thing. Many things contribute to the whole of a person, and just because vodka accounts for 50 percent of my body weight, that doesn't mean I walk around with a vodka drip, forcing every plant, person, or animal to imbibe. I've always had a disliking for animal trainers, and this guy cemented my theory that people who chaperone animals for a living have never had a girl sit on their face.

I went upstairs after my little incident with the Bruce photo and Googled "mini-horse." There turned out to be several Web sites and several mini-horses available for purchase, and I didn't need some animal trainer to approve the purchase. I learned that, just as with dwarfs, there was some sort of chromosomal deficiency that made these horses so small. I felt an instant connection to these miniature horses because of my work with Chuy, and I needed to have full access to one as soon as possible.

After more research I discovered that it is legal to have

a mini-horse as a house pet, as long as you have a backyard that meets certain measurements. Not only did my sister Sloane's yard meet the requirements, but she also had a little girl named Charley, along with a newborn named Russell, whose head Charley liked to squeeze on a semi-regular basis. This would be the perfect outlet for her to take her frustrations out on, allowing Sloane more time to figure out why all her babies were born with flat heads.

I called Sloane and gave her the news. "Charley can ride it all day long, and the only thing you have to do is get a fence in your backyard."

She went online to check out the horse and was ecstatic. "Oh, my God! They're so adorable! Why don't you get one?"

"Because, Sloane, I live in a building. I have no yard. They need to be ridden."

"But what about Buddy?"

Buddy was my sister's cat who had been missing for two years. "Sloane, Buddy is gone, and he's not coming back. He could be halfway to Arkansas by now."

"Well, he'd be way past Arkansas by now."

"You don't know that. You don't know what that cat's dreams were. He could have settled in the Midwest. What do you have against Middle America, Sloane?"

"First of all, he's on the Vineyard, because that's where we lost him, so unless he took the ferryboat across to the mainland, he's on the island. Mike and I are going to look again this summer."

"Well, good luck with that plan. In the meantime I see a mini-horse in your future."

Sloane and Mike losing their cat was as predictable in my view as Donny and Marie Osmond making love. They took the cat from a friend who was divorcing and moving into an apartment building that didn't allow animals. I liked the cat because he was significantly overweight and orange, my favorite color for cats, but it was still a cat and basically might as well have been an iguana. Charley terrorized the poor thing, always pulling on its tail and chasing it. The cat's new life sucked. I knew it, Sloane knew it, even my father knew it. "That cat's gonna head for the hills the minute he sees an opportunity. Don't take that cat to the Vineyard if you want to keep him. The very instant he sees the view from our house, he's going to want to live at the beach." The fact that cats hate water and the beach, and could therefore give two shits about an ocean view escaped him—another example of my father believing that anyone who set foot on his land would most surely want to take up full-time residence there.

"What if Buddy does come back, though, and the horse eats him?" Sloane asked me.

"Horses do not eat cats. Coyotes eat cats, and snakes eat cats. Snakes eat people, too, but we're losing focus—we're not getting you a snake. I'll get you the horse, we'll get a big fence to encompass your yard, and I think they just eat grass and hay, right? You'll have to clean up his dumps, which according to my research shouldn't be that massive, but that sounds like a job for Mike."

Chunk

We agreed I would move forward with the purchase of the mini-horse and have it sent to New Jersey. It was impossible to choose one because they were all so amazing, but I finally selected a little brown nugget horse whose name was Simon. I was hoping to come across one named Bruce, but there was no such luck. I called everyone I knew to tell them about the Web site. Ted, of course, thought the whole thing was a dumb idea. "They're going to get sick of that horse in a week, and Charley will poke it in the eye. The horse will be miserable, and so will Sloane. You don't get something just because it's cute, Chelsea. You have to think things through. This is why I'm never taking you to Africa."

Sloane called me the next day and told me Mike had said no to the horse, and she was starting to think it wasn't such a smart idea either.

"What are you talking about, Sloane? This horse is going to improve your quality of life! Charley will be busy every day riding him like a little cowgirl. You won't have to worry about her pulling Russell's ear off or trying to shove dinner rolls in his ass crack."

"I can't do it, Chelsea. I'm sorry. It just doesn't make any sense."

I didn't talk to Sloane for a few days, and for weeks afterward, every time I saw a horse or a cat, or a horse that looked like a cat, I was an emotional wreck.

I looked at Chunk, who was staring at the leftover hamburger meat in the Ziploc bag in my hand. "He's got an erection," I told Ted.

"Gross."

"Don't shame him! He has to know this is an open household where you can express yourself."

"Can you please tell me whose dog this is Chelsea?" he said, covering his eyes.

"I'm telling you, he's ours. He is part of our family now. It could be worse. What if I decided I wanted a baby? Then you'd really be fucked."

It took Ted a little while, but he finally realized Chunk was no joke and went over to pet him. "Well, what's his name?"

"Red Rocket," I said, staring straight at the dog's boner.

"Chelsea, what is his real name, please?"

"Chunk."

"I thought I was Chunk?" Ted asked. "That's going to confuse both of us. How am I going to know which one of us you're talking to?"

"From now on, Ted," I said, taking a seat at the kitchen table, "I will always be talking to the dog."

"That's great, Chelsea. Has he eaten?" he asked, eyeing the dog.

"Yes, I just made him some hamburger meat and steamed clams. He'll be fine until tomorrow. Eva is picking up some real dog food tomorrow."

"No, Chelsea! You cannot feed a dog clams! In the shell?"

"I can't?"

"Dogs can't eat human food, I'll go down to Ralphs and get him something," Ted volunteered. "I have a special recipe I do for dogs."

"Oh, really? I would like to hear that recipe."

"I do half dry food...and half Alpo," he said, waving his hands around like one of the guys on the tarmac with the orange sticks when your plane lands. I looked at him, walked into my bedroom, and shut the door. Then I opened it, let Chunk (the dog) in, and shut it again. I had no idea where or how to start explaining to Chunk what we were dealing with. How do you explain to a child that his father will try to feed him Alpo? I didn't even know Alpo was still in business, and I certainly didn't know Ted was on their board of directors.

As if this weren't bad enough, the next morning Ted schooled me in dog training. I was in the shower, and Chunk was standing outside, chivalrously looking away while I put my body through a rinse cycle. Ted walked in, said good morning to the dog, then put his hand above Chunk's head and pushed it through the air. He instructed Chunk to "Sit!"—which Chunk did on command. "Chelsea, this is how you to tell a dog to sit," he announced.

I hadn't even finished lathering my shampoo into my hair when I kicked open the shower door. "Oh, really, Dog Whisperer? Is that how you do it?"

"You know what, Chelsea? How am *I* supposed to know if *you* know dog tricks?" he said, throwing up his hands in hopelessness.

"Are you being serious right now, Ted? I really must know."

"Chelsea, you don't even like dogs."

"Telling a dog how to sit is not only *not* a trick, it's probably the single most universal thing in the world, aside from army salutes and brownies." I wished my new dog didn't have to be subjected to this kind of humiliation, but this was his life now, and he needed to know what we were up against. We would be in this together, and I felt relieved to have an ally. Someone who understood me, loved me, and didn't know how to disagree with me.

When I told my sister Sidney about the new addition to my family, she said, "This sounds a little overwhelming for someone with your limited skill set, Chelsea. You've already killed three fish. Have you thought about putting Ted down?"

"I told you Ted said those fish were starter fish who were sacrificing their lives to stabilize our aquarium and then we'd get pretty fish. Why do you keep bringing that up?"

After word spread that I'd gotten a dog, I received some of the most annoying e-mails I've ever encountered. Friends wanting to know if I wanted to arrange doggy play dates, lists of dog parks in my area, advice on what food to feed him, how to socialize him—essentially a collection of people I decided to end friendships with. The only doggy activity I was prepared to do was doggy style, and I'd be lying if I said that hadn't lost its appeal sometime around my sweet sixteen. I always thought people were annoying with their baby advice, but this seemed like it might be worse. I had spent my entire life with one dog or another, and aside from being emotionally unstable, each family dog we had seemed like a pretty cut-and-dried case. They started out as puppies, grew up, and then died, in no specific order.

The one person I allow to take Chunk for overnight visits is my friend Michael. He is a gay man with his own dog and is obsessed with Chunk and insists on calling him "Chunkity Chunk." He has Chunk every Saturday for an overnight slumber party and then reports back to me on Sunday how he and Chunk talked for hours and that dogs are really the only people who understand him.

"I have a special language that dogs understand," he'll tell me in his deep Texan twang. "He'll lie on top of me, and I'll give him a forty-five-minute deep-tissue massage, and he looooooooves it. Then I'll turn on your TV show and watch it, and Chunk will sit down right in front of the TV and stare straight at you. He loves the show! He is such a special dog, Chelsea. I just have such a love for him. He is so funny!"

It's pointless trying to tell Michael that dogs aren't funny, simply because they are dogs and they are incapable of telling jokes or getting them, for that matter. It's pointless to tell Michael much of anything because he is in a world all his own and he has the attention span of an espresso maker. He also has a pretty unhealthy, though seemingly innocuous, relationship with his own dog.

I wanted to make sure there was nothing going on with Chunk that I would be alarmed by. "You're not putting your finger in my dog's asshole, right?" I asked him one afternoon on the phone. I didn't really believe that he was, but I had just finished Mia Farrow's autobiography and I didn't want to be one of those mothers who let their child hang out with a Woody Allen type who was doing inappropriate things to their flesh and blood.

"Chelsea Handler, I would never, ever put my finger in any dog's asshole. I wouldn't hurt any animal on this earth for all the money in the world. I love dogs, and I love Chunk, and I think you know that I would never hurt a fly."

"That's not the point, Michael. You can never fit your finger into a fly's asshole."

"Chelsea, please don't do this."

"Okay, sorry. As a mother, I just had to ask."

"I understand," Michael told me. "I do think Chunk is gay, though. And also I want to be put in your will just in case you die, so that I get Chunk. Ted won't care, right?"

Michael still takes Chunk every weekend, and I know he doesn't stick anything in his asshole, because Chunk gets so excited every time Michael shows up to take him. And I know Chunk is straight because he tested negative for the gay virus.

Chunk still follows me around all the time, but he has chilled out a little bit, mostly because he saw the toll it was taking on me when Ted did the same thing. Once in a while, Ted and I will forget to put food away and then come home to find the remains of a wheel of Brie spread across our duvet and Chunk passed out next to the bed. It happens only every so often, but when it does, our entire condo smells like a foot and I'm convinced that my mother has reincarnated herself as Chunk. Spreading Brie over my bedspread and coming back to life as a dog is totally something my mother would do.

To this day Chunk has still not taken a dump in front of me, and I respect him for it. I always said I would never get a dog until they came out with one that either doesn't take a dump or knows how to bartend. The fact that Chunk has no problem taking a dump in front of Ted makes me respect him more. I hope that one day soon the two of them can take dumps together.

My dog, Chunk

Chapter Eleven

Deep Thoughts by
Chelsea Handy

My tendency to make up stories and lie compulsively for the sake of my own amusement takes up a good portion of my day and provides me with a peace of mind not easily attainable in this economic climate. The following is a catalog of lies that have been left open-ended, and in all these instances, the victims have not been made aware that they have fallen prey to complete and utter nonsense. "Dumbassness" is the word I would use to describe the condition they suffer from.

SILLY SULLY

My friend Stephanie believes that Sully, the pilot who landed the US Airways flight in the Hudson River, is currently Ted's and my personal pilot. We had arrived in Turks and Caicos a day after Stephanie, on a regular plane like everyone else. That night at dinner, Ted mentioned the turbulence on the flight and casually mentioned that had Sully been our pilot, he would have been a lot less stressed. Stephanie was sitting a couple of seats down and asked me if she heard correctly.

"Did I hear you say Sully, the guy who landed that plane, was your pilot?"

"He's an American hero is what he is," I told her.

"I know he is!" she exclaimed. "How did that happen?"

"Ted called and offered him a bunch of money," I told her. "Apparently he's a huge fan of the E! network and *Keeping Up with the Kardashians.* He now provides this service for a lot of people. We're third on his list. So if no one else is flying that day, we get him. He's a pretty interesting guy."

"That is so cool!" Stephanie exclaimed, while everyone else at the table was rolling their eyes except for my brother Ray, who has always been a little slow on the uptake.

Ted got up from his seat and moved down to the other side of the table while I explained to Stephanie that Ted isn't the best flier and Sully has basically become a member of our family. "He and Ted go golfing together all the time. He was supposed to come on this trip, but Beyoncé needed him tomorrow. He says she uses the ThighMaster the entire flight. She just sits there working out her thighs for hours straight while Jay-Z raps."

"Oh, my God!" Steph cried. "She is such a mess!"

My friend Paul was sitting across from me, shaking his head and pretending to be texting on his BlackBerry. Eva piped up. "Sometimes he lets Ted sit in the cockpit."

"That is so cool. Ted must feel like one of the Beatles! Who else is on the list before you?" Steph asked.

"That's so funny you just said the Beatles because it's actually Beyoncé and Sir Paul McCartney."

Stephanie stopped chewing her food. "Shut up."

I never told Stephanie I was kidding, and sometime later, when I was flying out for a stand-up show in Atlantic City, she texted me on the way to the airport and asked if I was flying with Sully.

"Yup. He just texted me that he got *Marley & Me* for the flight. How cute is that?"

"I want to meet him! Also, see if you can get any more dish on Beyoncé and Jay-Z," she wrote.

"I already did. Apparently, Beyoncé has to load up an entire separate plane for her wardrobe because Sully hates the House of Deréon and thinks Beyoncé's mother is trying to exploit her own daughter with her tacky designs. Sully refuses to do it. He's way in on the drama."

"Who knew a pilot from Pennsylvania would have such

a good eye?" she responded. "Please keep me in the loop. Invite him to your birthday this year. He sounds like one of us."

"I'm on it," I typed back. As for my brother, I'm unclear if he even knew who we were talking about, since there's a chance he entirely missed the news story about Sully landing on the Hudson in the first place.

THE *CHALLENGER*

A year ago I told one of the writers on my staff, Heather McDonald, that I was being offered the main role in a movie about Christa McCauliffe and the *Challenger* space shuttle blowing up. Heather is by far the most gullible person on my staff, and all the writers on the show are constantly making up ridiculous stories to tell her just for the sake of our own amusement. She's not stupid; she just seems to love anything involving free items, money, or drama.

"The weird part," I told her, "is that it's a comedy, and they're allowing me to hire my own writer to write my part." This was enough to pique Heather's interest and motivate her to put some ideas together and get a head start before some of the other writers came up with anything substantial. "Meryl Streep is playing Christa McCauliffe," I added, "but she's dead and only comes down from heaven to talk to me in the movie."

My partner Tom walked into my office halfway through

this debacle and took no time to jump in and add his own spin. "Chelsea plays her daughter, who grew up never knowing her mother and is now married and in the process of becoming an astronaut. But every time she gets into a space shuttle, she has terrible flashbacks about the day."

"Are you going to do it?" Heather asked me.

"Yes, obviously, I want to! Meryl Streep? I can't pass that up. And they have an offer out to Hank Azaria to play my husband."

"That's so weird." She sat on the sofa in my office looking at me. "How can they make this a comedy?"

"That's where you come in, Heather," Tom told her. "We're going to have all the writers submit ideas for the story line, since the studio is willing to hire a personal writer from Chelsea's staff to outline the story. They definitely want it to have a comedic twist."

"It's so weird that they would make it a comedy," she said. "That was a really horrible event."

"It is weird," I agreed. "It's downright creepy, but who am I to take a moral stand on someone else's vision? That's why I need help. I'm going to ask all the writers to come up with an outline for the movie and some really funny scenes. Apparently there's going to be a lot of improv. Meryl loves improv, I guess, and never really gets to do it."

"She does?"

"Yes," Tom assured her. "I've seen her talk about it on *Inside the Actors Studio.* She feels robbed."

"Well, it is a good subject for a movie. I mean, everyone

remembers where they were that day. I remember when they announced that the *Challenger* blew up. I was in fifth or sixth grade, I think," she said.

"Yeah, I remember, too. Although I was younger, of course."

"So basically," Tom interjected, "you need to write a few pages of dialogue and/or plotlines and submit them along with the other writers, and then we're going to decide who will make the seventy-five-thousand-dollar writing fee."

"Seventy-five thousand dollars?" Heather asked.

"At least," he told her. "Could even turn out to be more. How soon can you get something to us?"

"I'll start working on it this weekend," she said. "Is there any other information you can give me?"

"Well," I told her, "my husband in the movie hates for me to be in space. He just wants me to do something where I spend the majority of time on earth. There's actually a scene where I shit my pants in a space-shuttle simulator." I looked at Tom, who had turned around and was going through my belts. "I already told her they have an offer out to Hank Azaria to play my husband."

"No," Tom corrected me. "Actually, the last I heard was that he passed and they were going in a different direction. They were going to make an offer to Justin Timberlake, who they say is interested."

"Shut up!" Heather wailed.

"No way!" I exclaimed, jumping out of my seat. "I *have* to do it now."

"You have to do it. Let me start brainstorming." She got up to go to her office. "One last thing—do they have a title?" she asked me.

"Yes," Tom told her. "It's called *The Sky Is Crying*."

TURKS AND CAICOS

At some point during our vacation, Sylvan asked me if my friend Paul was gay, which he is. Instead of giving him a straightforward answer, I saw an opportunity and told Sylvan that not only was Paul gay but that he was actually still a woman who was currently going through gender-reassignment surgery. He was raised as a boy until he was eighteen and started dating a girl. He found out that boy parts are different from girl parts and that he had the exact same parts as his girlfriend. Gender reassignment is a pretty laborious process, so each month he got estrogen injections, and his body had been slowly transforming his girl parts into male parts. After this trip he was getting his penis.

"Holy shit, Chels." Sylvan was horrified. "What happened to the girl?"

"She was freaked out," I told him. "She enlisted in the military immediately after he told her and has since been deployed to Iraq."

"So he has girl parts right now?"

"Yes. He has a clitoris, but after this vacation is when they inject him with the hormones to enlarge the clitoris into a full-blown penis."

"Why didn't he want to stay being a girl?"

"Because he spent his whole life thinking he was a boy and associates more with boys. If you look closely at his tits, you can see that they used to be bigger."

"Oh, my God, Chels." Sylvan was rubbing his head. "I've never heard of anything like this."

"Yup. What they do is give you pills to basically turn your clitoris into a penis. Pretty fucked up, huh?"

Sylvan and I were on a boat watching Paul swim around with a snorkel, looking for fish. "He looks so much like a guy," Sylvan said.

"I know. It's taken a lot of work for him to get there. He used to have hair longer than mine. It's amazing to actually watch the transformation. His body has been through so many stages. At least now people think he's a *guy*. There was a time not long ago when you couldn't tell what he was."

Sylvan was flabbergasted, and I was having the time of my life. He was still rubbing his head as if he were in pain and asked me, "So is he technically a boy or a girl right now?"

"Right now he's both. His parents, wanting a boy, decided that even though he had a coslopus, they would raise him as a boy. After he found out he was a girl, he got into real estate, because he knew that was the quickest way to make a buck, and he's been saving money ever since to make 'the change.'"

"But, Chels, he looks and talks and walks like a guy," Sylvan told me.

"I know, Sylvan. Medicine is amazing," I declared. "A-mazing, His real name is Bernice, but his parents just called him Bernie, and then when he found out that they were lying to him his whole life, he changed his name to Paul."

Sylvan couldn't stop asking questions. Luckily, I had an answer for each one. When Paul came in after snorkeling, Sylvan got up and handed him a towel. He also started pulling out Paul's seat each night at dinner, which clearly confused Paul every time, but was enjoyable for me to watch.

"I don't get it, Chels," Sylvan asked. "Does he like girls or boys?"

"Boys."

"But if he likes boys, wouldn't it have been easier to just stay a girl, instead of becoming a man and then becoming gay?"

"That's a pretty good fucking question, Sylvan," I told him. "One that I ask myself every day when I look at Paul's ass. It's hard to understand the transgender community and what their thoughts are. Why they want to cross two hurdles instead of one, but I don't ask questions, Sylvan. I don't judge. I'm not the Lord."

At the end of the trip, Sylvan told Paul that he was one of the most amazing people he'd ever met and that Paul had more guts and courage than half those soldiers who go over to Iraq.

"Thank you, Sylvan," Paul said quizzically. "That's a really nice thing to say to someone. I think."

"Gosh," Eva remarked to Paul. "You must really have made an impression on him."

Paul told me after that that he felt bad for judging Sylvan based on the fact that he couldn't swim. "That guy's a sweetheart through and through. You should have heard what he told me when we said good-bye. I'm definitely going to use him as a driver the next time I'm in New York.

"You should definitely use him," I told him.

IKE TURNER

On the same trip, Paul and I got into a food fight one night around three in the morning. This is something we frequently participate in after seven to ten cocktails. We are respectful enough to do it only in the privacy of our hotel room, and I usually end up the champion, as Paul is gay, which can lead to terrible hand-eye coordination. While we don't intentionally involve others, it usually requires anyone else in the room to run and duck for cover, as it can get pretty violent, with one or two fruit items ending up stuck to a wall and Paul screaming that I'm an angry dyke. I'm more apt to fight with Paul instead of someone like Tanya, because I consider Paul to be more of an equal and Tanya to be more of a mad harlot.

Things got particularly hairy one night on our vacation in Turks and Caicos, and fruit throwing eventually graduated from grapes and decorative acorns to ripe nectarines. When I turned around to peg a strawberry in Paul's direction, I didn't have time to duck before a nectarine hit me square in the eye. It hurt, but not enough to make me cry, and I quickly recovered, although all our other friends were a little taken aback at our level of violence.

Ted scolded us both: "Stop it, you two! Chelsea has a television show, and I already gave her one black eye when we were playing Wii tennis. People are going to think I beat her."

Sylvan was more impressed with Paul's hand-eye

coordination, because at that point he didn't know if Paul was a boy, a girl, or a sea animal.

Either way, the party came to a screeching halt with Paul really concerned that he'd hurt me. He hadn't, but when I woke up the next morning, my friend Stephanie suggested that it would be a good idea to have me fake a black eye. With Eva and Stephanie's help, I was able to make one side of my face look like Rihanna's, and then I headed down in the bright sunlight with a hat and sunglasses, like any respectful abused woman.

My brother, Delicious, Ted, Paul, and Sylvan were all down at breakfast already when the girls and I arrived. When Paul caught on to my face, he was horrified. I assured him it was no big deal and that I had time to heal before I had to tape the show again. "Don't worry," I told him. "I bruise easily. If it's still there by Monday, I'm sure my makeup artist can cover it up. Or I'll just tell the audience my friend hit me with a nectarine."

"You should take iron," Ted told me as he got up from the table, giving me a thumbs-up for my cosmetic handiwork. Ted was in our room that morning when I applied my shiner and was excited to be included in a joke. "Good job, Paul," Ted told him, and threw his napkin down on the table dramatically before heading over to his beach chair.

Not knowing that it was a joke, Sylvan was disgusted by the whole event. He said to Paul, "If you weren't a girl, I would have the right mind to hit you," and then he stormed off. Brian, Ray, and Paul all looked at each other, wondering what Sylvan was talking about, until I explained to them that Sylvan didn't have a ton of experience with gay men and that calling men girls was just English slang for gay guys.

Shortly after, I explained to Sylvan that the whole thing was a joke, that Paul really hadn't hurt me and to just go along with it. He was bellowing with laughter. "Chels, you are a maniac! I can't believe I fell for that. And what an idiot he is, too, for believing it!"

"I know," I said to Sylvan. "Can you believe how stupid everyone is?"

As the day wore on, Eva, Steph, and I kept making the bruise darker and darker, until finally Paul took me aside with tears in his eyes.

Paul is gay with an exorbitant amount of energy and an annoyingly sunny disposition. He has the tendency to look at every situation as a glass half gay and is the type of person who says "Bless his heart" when he sees someone in a wheelchair getting off a ski lift.

"Chelsea," he whimpered, "I just feel terrible. You are so generous to all of us, and you have been such a good friend, and I thank you by hitting you in the face with a nectarine, and look at you, you look awful."

"Don't worry about it, Paul. I'm seriously not mad at you. I know it was a total accident." When tears started to fill his gay eyes, I took a towel and wetted it with a bottle of water. "Look," I told him, "it will probably just wipe off."

With Stephanie's video camera capturing the event,

including the disappearance of the bruise, Paul realized what I had done. "You are horrible!" he screamed. "Horrible! You're a horrible, angry dyke!"

ONE-LEGGED WONDER

A while back I tried to set my friend Sarah up with my brother Ray, to no avail.

"Whatever happened to hooking him up with Sarah?" Sloane asked me when my sisters and I were on a three-way phone call discussing the fact that our brother had been single for far too long.

"It's a little late for that, since she's getting married in two weeks. I do love Ray, and I'd be willing to break up most relationships if it meant giving him one, but I have grown to love Sarah's fiancé, even though Firouz is Iranian and has only one leg."

"Come again?" Sidney asked me.

"I told you guys this already," I lied.

"No, Chelsea. I think I would have remembered if you told me that Sarah's fiancé was legless. Is he in a wheelchair?"

"No. I really can't believe I didn't tell you this already. He lost one of his legs in Iraq."

"I thought he was an editor?" Sloane asked.

"He is," I confirmed. "But he volunteered for the war and lost his leg in combat, so he's got one of those plastic thingamijiggies."

242

"Sarah is marrying someone with no leg?" Sidney asked.

"He has one leg. God, you guys are pretty judgmental. He loves her and she loves him. It's not like he can't walk around."

"So let me get this straight," Sloane asked. "She rejected Ray for a one-legged soldier? Is he a Republican, too?"

"No! Of course not! He's a Democrat."

"Where is the leg?" inquired Sloane.

"I have no idea where the leg is, Sloane. This isn't *CSI: Miami*. I didn't ask where the leg is. Obviously it's gone. It's probably still somewhere in Afghanistan."

"Chelsea, you said Iraq," Sidney reminded me. "Is this one of your stupid stories? Because it sure sounds stupid."

"Then ask her!" I yelled, exhausted. "Like I'd make up someone losing their leg."

A week later Ray moved out to Los Angeles to be the caterer for my show. He had come to learn about Firouz's leg through my sisters and had questions of his own. Sarah was nice enough to invite Ray to her wedding, since he was new to L.A., and when Ray watched Sarah and Firouz dance to their first song, he leaned over and said to Ted, "For a guy with one leg, *that guy* can really move. Are Iranians known for dancing?"

It didn't take long for Ted to come over and inform me that not only did he confirm my lie about Firouz's having one leg, but he also took it up a notch and told Ray that Firouz was able to score Heather Mills's old leg on eBay for only fifteen hundred dollars. Not an amazing attempt to corroborate my story, but a valiant effort nonetheless, especially for someone who took so long to get on board with my chronic storytelling. I was just glad we were finally on the same team. Like Serena and Venus playing doubles together. Not opponents but large black teammates.

The End

Acknowledgments

These are the people I acknowledge: Michael Broussard, Beth de Guzman, Jamie Raab, Sara Weiss, Anne Twomey, Grand Central Publishing, Hachette Book Group, and the main person involved in getting everyone to give away all of their rights: Eva Magdalenski from Denver. My sisters and brothers for giving me a life; it's safe to say your efforts in me paid off. I acknowledge my father, although I don't appreciate his body type or complete lack of morality. Steve Marmalstein, Jen Kirkman, Heather McDonald, Johnny Milord, Chris Franjola, Sarah Colonna, Brad Wollack, Jeff Wild, Guy Branum, and Sue Murphy for carrying me when I am too tired to carry myself, like footprints in the sand but not really. Tom Brunelle is responsible for me having any time to write a book, and responsible for allowing me to sleep in, and responsible for me having a successful mid-level cable show. I love you, dearly. Also, thank you, India. And finally, thank you Belvedere Vodka for keeping me sane.